Entrepreneur MAGAZINE'S

startup

Start Your Own

VENDING BUSINESS

Your Step-by-Step Guide to Success

Anne Rawland Gabriel

EP
Entrepreneur
Press

Editorial Director: Jere L. Calmes
Managing Editor: Marla Markman
Cover Design: Beth Hansen-Winter
Production: Eliot House Productions
Composition: Ed Stevens

This publication is designed to provide accurate and authoritative information in regard to
the subject matter covered. It is sold with the understanding that the publisher is not
engaged in rendering legal, accounting, or other professional services. If legal advice or
other expert assistance is required, the services of a competent professional person should be
sought.

Library of Congress Cataloging-in-Publication Data
Gabriel, Anne Rowland.
    Start your own vending business/by Anne Rowland Gabriel.
        p.   cm.   —(Entrepreneur magazine's start up)
    Includes index.
    ISBN 1-891984-85-3
        1. Vending machine. 2. New business enterprises—Management. 3.
Entrepreneurship. I. Title. II. Series.

HF5483.G33 2003
658.8'7—dc21   2003043950

Printed in Canada

09 08 07 06 05   10 9 8 7 6 5 4

Contents

Preface

If you're reading this, you're most likely interested in starting a vending business or at least finding out more about what owning one would be like. Either way, we know from experience just what you need.

You need information, but not written in a manner that causes you to nod off. You need facts, but not every fact that's out there—only the ones that'll get you up and running. You need advice, but only the best and most relevant in the land. And you need reassurance that the leap you're about to take is more than just one of faith.

So let's start with that last bit first. Indeed, you're repeatedly going to hear how much work owning a business is and how difficult it is to be successful. However, this country was founded on the principle of controlling one's own destiny and being one's own boss. While some folks focus on the negative, we'd like to stress the positive: Owning a business is a tradition in this country, and you can be proud to be a part of it.

As for the rest of what you need, we've sifted through literally piles of information and spent hours talking to successful entrepreneurs and industry experts. Many of the messages we heard were repeated over and over by people who don't even know each other. We've taken all that data and distilled it into a solid source of information for you.

In addition, you'll find in the Glossary all the lingo you'll need to speak like a pro as well as contact information in the Appendix for everyone we spoke to. If there's one common theme we heard again and again, it's to call on those with experience—they'll be happy to help answer your questions and give you additional advice.

One problem with this book is that it suffers the limitation of any two-dimensional resource. The written word requires taking a very nonlinear world and putting it into a linear format. While we've put lots of thought into organizing the flow of topics in a logical fashion, reading each page in sequence may not work for you.

Instead, we encourage you to jump around as much as you like, seeking out related information when you're ready to learn it. We'd even encourage you to flip first to Chapter 16 for some of the most valuable advice you'll find between these covers.

After you're finished with the last chapter, consider skipping next to Chapter 2, where you'll learn whether vending is the glamorous affair you've always imagined or perhaps not quite for you. Then, if you're still with us, start in again from the beginning and work your way through.

No matter how you use this book—whether you read it cover to cover or simply refer to it as questions arise—we know it'll serve you well as you embark on what's sure to be one of the most exhilarating experiences of your life: being your own boss.

Finally, we'd like to tell you upfront that the business owners and experts we interviewed gave most generously of time, energy, and resources. They also provided this book's sample forms, documents, worksheets, etc., which you're sure to find invaluable for adapting to your own business needs. It's to them that we owe our most sincere gratitude for making this guide possible.

So sit back, get comfortable, and let your journey begin.

1

Introduction

Before investing time, energy, money, and, most important, yourself in any business, it's just plain good sense to know something about what you're getting into. History, current issues, and future trends all impact the steps you take toward becoming a successful entrepreneur.

Photo© Automatic Products International Ltd.

And in the case of this book, it's also important to know who's giving you the advice. Do they have similar backgrounds? Are their towns similar to yours? How do their businesses compare to the one you're planning to start?

The more you know, the more likely you are to prosper. So without further ado, let's answer the questions we've already asked as well as a few more.

What Are We Talking About?

If you visit your American Heritage dictionary, you'll likely discover the definition of vending machine is "a coin-operated machine that dispenses merchandise." Of course, if you've purchased food, beverages, or sundries from a vending machine lately, you know paper money and, in some areas, plastic are also involved.

Perhaps a more thorough description of vending is the one suggested by the National Automatic Merchandising Association (NAMA) in its booklet, *Vending 101*: "the business of buying, placing on location, filling with product, removing cash, and maintaining vending equipment."

Like boiling down the theory of gravity to "what goes up must come down," the day-to-day realities of a successful vending operation are a bit more sophisticated. But NAMAs definition is an excellent place to start.

Where It All Began

According to *A Concise History of Vending* by respected professor, prolific author, and NAMA President Emeritus G. Richard Schreiber, the earliest known vending machine was an Egyptian liquid-distribution device dating from 215 B.C. Not surprisingly, the device dispensed holy water at places of worship when a coin was deposited.

In the United States, it is generally accepted that vending began in 1888, when the Adams Gum company introduced its penny machines. From this humble beginning, vending has grown to an industry with gross sales estimated between $24 billion and $34 billion.

Current State of Affairs

For years and years, food-related vending enjoyed unbridled growth as factories and offices sprang up across North America. Even today, food remains the largest vending segment at about 93 percent of the industry, according to trade news journal *Vending Times*.

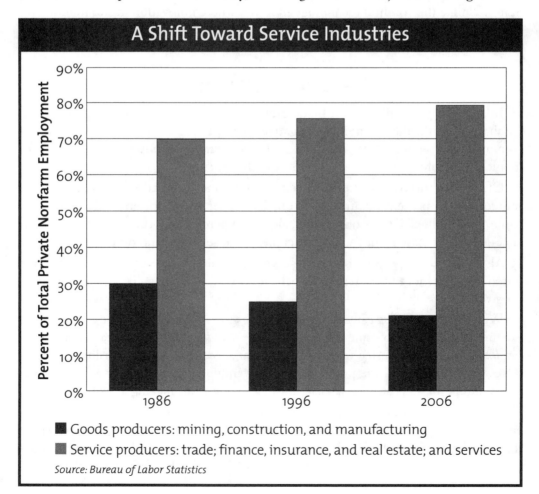

A Shift Toward Service Industries

Percent of Total Private Nonfarm Employment

■ Goods producers: mining, construction, and manufacturing
■ Service producers: trade; finance, insurance, and real estate; and services

Source: Bureau of Labor Statistics

But the extensive NAMA-commissioned report by Hudson Analytics, *The Future of the Vending and Foodservice Industry 1998–2013*, points out downsizing, the shift from a manufacturing to a service economy, and the rise of telecommuting have reined in the industry. Over the past decade, the vending industry's share of total food sales dropped sharply from 2.7 to 1.4 percent.

At the same time, other types of vending have appeared. For instance, telecard vending exploded onto the market in the 1990s. Continued growth in this segment is expected as consumer usage of prepaid phone cards climbs above 50 percent early this century, say reports in *Vending Times*.

Other types of specialty vending—everything from pizza and french fries to pantyhose and office supplies—are also on the rise, but verifiable statistics on the strength of these sectors are not yet available.

Although consumers in countries like Japan buy an ever-expanding array of vended products, vending is generally considered to be a "mature" industry in the United States. Unlike the youthful technology industry, where innovation makes millionaires overnight, today's keys to vending success are cost control, aggressive marketing, exceptional management, and a lot of plain hard work.

Hazards to Navigate

In addition to hurdles posed by tangible economic forces, vending continues to combat a significant intangible—negative perceptions. Another recent NAMA-commissioned report, *Management Report: What Consumers Think of Vending*, by Techmonic Inc., explored consumer attitudes toward vending.

Of those who do purchase from vending machines (instead of from some other source), only 1 percent identify "high quality" as the motivator and only 16 percent name "good value." On the other hand, almost 64 percent report being a captive audience—they purchase from vending machines because there is no other alternative.

Also, nearly 20 percent of those surveyed believe most vending machines are unreliable, and more than 70 percent believe it's difficult to get a refund if something goes wrong.

While the underlying causes of these findings were beyond the scope of the report, explanations are easy to come by. *Automatic Merchandiser* (a monthly trade magazine), *Vending Times*, and industry watchers in general agree that vending businesses themselves are the source of the problem. During vending's heydays of growth and prosperity, attending to customer satisfaction was irrelevant to making a profit.

Another factor contributing to consumers' negative image of vending will be discussed in more detail in Chapter 3. To summarize: Scams in vending are so prevalent that hundreds, if not thousands, of innocent individuals are sold vending machines every year under false but convincing pretenses. Typically, the victims of such schemes place machines at various locations, slowly go bankrupt, and then simply abandon the equipment, leaving the consumers frustrated and without recourse.

Back to the Future

Before you close this book and give up your dream in despair, we want you to know the picture isn't entirely black. The Hudson report shows that various technological, economic, demographic, and other forces are opening doors to new ways of doing business and new markets to explore.

For example, cellular telephones and pagers reduce vending businesses' overhead by decreasing the need for secretarial support. Laptops, at larger operations, and palmtops allow for inputting information directly rather than scribbling down machine-fill data and crunching numbers later by hand.

On the economic side, more two-income families mean increased demand for home-meal replacements as well as new opportunities for product differentiation.

Demographically, the newest consumers, Generations X and Y, have been profoundly affected by the forces discussed previously. Becoming more self-reliant at a younger age than their parents, they started preparing their own meals and making their own purchasing decisions early in life. One result the Hudson report points out is that snacking and "grazing" are norms for both groups, while three sit-down meals daily are the exception.

> **Fun Fact**
> Generation Xers are big consumers of handheld foods, according to a recent Hudson Analytics report, *The Future of the Vending and Foodservice Industry 1998–2013.* Fifty-eight percent of Gen Xers surveyed selected sandwiches or bagels for lunch.

What's It All Mean?

Admittedly, the swiftly changing landscape is making the process of doing business particularly difficult for established vending organizations that are accustomed to doing everything "the old way." In addition to the Hudson report, articles in *Automatic Merchandiser*, reports in *Vending Times*, and statements by organizations like NAMA repeatedly admonish vending companies to pay more attention to merchandising, customer service, computerization, and related efficiencies.

In other words, just filling machines isn't good enough anymore.

For entrepreneurs like you, the current and future trends of the industry offer as many opportunities as roadblocks. Unfettered by "the way we've always done it," you can turn the challenges of the rapidly changing marketplace to your advantage faster than can an established organization, where old habits often die hard.

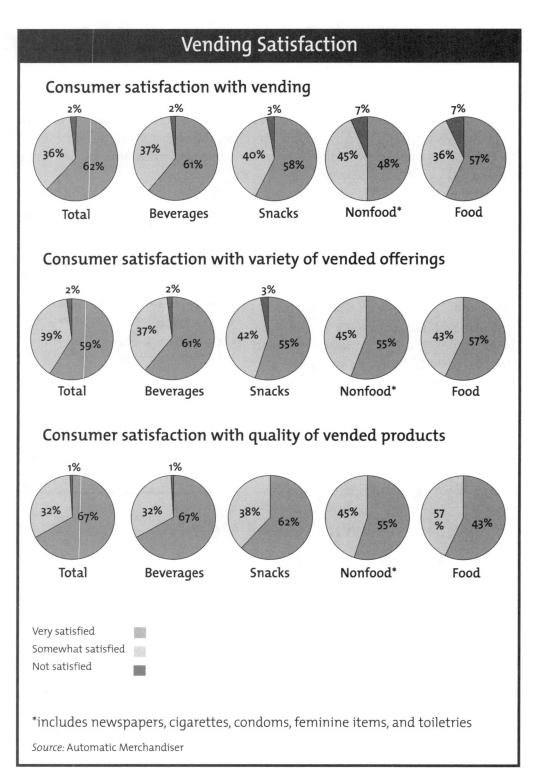

Vending Satisfaction

Consumer satisfaction with vending

Total	Beverages	Snacks	Nonfood*	Food
2% / 36% / 62%	2% / 37% / 61%	3% / 40% / 58%	7% / 45% / 48%	7% / 36% / 57%

Consumer satisfaction with variety of vended offerings

Total	Beverages	Snacks	Nonfood*	Food
2% / 39% / 59%	2% / 37% / 61%	3% / 42% / 55%	45% / 55%	43% / 57%

Consumer satisfaction with quality of vended products

Total	Beverages	Snacks	Nonfood*	Food
1% / 32% / 67%	1% / 32% / 67%	38% / 62%	45% / 55%	57% / 43%

Very satisfied
Somewhat satisfied
Not satisfied

*includes newspapers, cigarettes, condoms, feminine items, and toiletries

Source: Automatic Merchandiser

This Work's Focus

To help you become a successful operator, this book draws on the insights of entrepreneurs who took advantage of opportunities by entering relatively new vending fields or embracing the forces of innovation and change. It also provides insights from those who watched countless wanna-bes and savvy survivors.

Because consumable products dominate the profit potential in the vending industry and offer you the best opportunities, we'll focus on this segment. We'll also introduce you to issues faced by entrepreneurs who identify an unexplored vending market and strike off to conquer the unknown.

Other Opportunities

What's not specifically addressed here is amusement vending—arcade games, jukeboxes, etc.—and street vending. Bulk vending—stickers, toys, and gumballs—and office coffee service (OCS) are also underrepresented.

In the case of amusement and street vending, many of the basics of vending consumables apply. Even more information will apply to bulk vending and OCS, but their segments also face issues beyond the scope of this work.

For those interested in the foregoing, we recommend using this business guide to acquaint yourself with the fundamentals and as a valuable source for worksheets and checklists. In addition, you will find references to more specific assistance listed in the Appendix.

Meet Our Operators

Vending business owners most often refer to themselves as "operators," a term we've wholeheartedly adopted. We'll supply you with all the jargon you'll need to navigate the industry in the next chapter and our Glossary, but for now, we'd like to introduce you to the voices you'll hear throughout this book.

Wayne D. of Burnsville, Minnesota, a suburb of Minneapolis, is our most veteran entrepreneur. He started his business part time in 1978 while still working as a full-time cigarette vending sales representative for tobacco company R.J. Reynolds. "I was nearing 40 and knew I wasn't going to be retiring with Reynolds," says Wayne.

Wayne chose vending because his Reynolds job gave him a bird's-eye view of what worked and what didn't. "I had a distinct advantage

> **Fun Fact**
> Vending is an entrepreneur's business, according to the National Automatic Merchandising Association. More than 75 percent of the companies in the industry have sales of less than $1 million.

because I saw how two or three hundred companies operated," he explains. "So my wife and I started our company with 14 candy, snack, and cigarette machines in five different locations." Five years and a number of smaller acquisitions later, Wayne purchased a larger operation and traded his Reynolds position for working in vending full time.

Janice M. of Baltimore represents entrepreneurship in its truest sense. "In May of 1995, I had a job interview at 8:30 A.M.," says the 30-ish single African-American mother of three. "After dropping off my children, I arrived for the interview at 12 minutes after eight, and I suddenly noticed I had a hole the size of Seattle in my pantyhose."

Although the receptionist directed her to the company canteen, by the time she found the hosiery, selected between beige, gray, or black, negotiated the checkout counter, and returned to the waiting area, time had run out. "I was told I didn't have time to put them on," Janice recalls. "Well, this was my first real corporate job and I wanted to make a good impression, so I didn't want to be late."

Janice figures her boss must have noticed the gaping crevasse, but he never uttered a word and offered her the administrative assistant position anyway. For the next year she revisited the incident several times. "I remember I just kept thinking about it—I

Market Share of Vended Products

Cold drinks (cans)	41.6%
Snacks and pastries (packaged)	19.4%
Hot drinks	8.1%
Refrigerated/frozen foods	7.1%
Cold drinks (cups)	6.2%
Cold drinks (bottles)	5.7%
Cigarettes and cigars	3.6%
Milk	1.4%
Juice (dedicated vendors)*	1.9%
Ice cream	1.3%
Bulk	1.0%
Hot canned food	0.4%
All other	2.5%
Total	**100.2%**

*Juice is also sold through other beverage vendors, such as canned soda or bottled drink machines.

Source: Vending Times' most recent census of the industry. Total equals more than 100 percent due to rounding. Percentages for each category fluctuate somewhat from year to year.

don't know why. But I kept thinking it would have been really great if there had been a machine in the bathroom so I didn't have to go running around."

While she worked as an administrative assistant, Janice ran an event-planning business on the side and enrolled in a business training class offered by a local economic development organization: Women Entrepreneurs of Baltimore. She mentioned the idea to a fellow classmate, and he suggested she go to the library and research the subject in *Vending Times*.

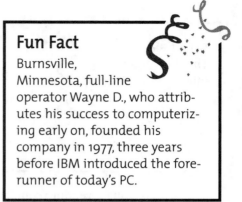

Fun Fact

Burnsville, Minnesota, full-line operator Wayne D., who attributes his success to computerizing early on, founded his company in 1977, three years before IBM introduced the forerunner of today's PC.

"*Vending Times* didn't have anything listed that was solely pantyhose, so I called vending companies to see if anyone had heard of it," Janice recollects. But no one had. So Janice decided to give the idea a go, and by midsummer 1996, her business was born.

Because she's not only pitching vending but the concept of pantyhose dispensing as well, Janice still works in the corporate world part time. But she remains optimistic and focused on her dream of concentrating on her business full time and even franchising her patented idea. "I just want to make a lasting impression for years to come," she asserts, "so that my children can grow up and say, 'This is something Mommy did, and we can do it, too.'"

Becky P. of Northridge, California, launched into vending full time in 1984 when she and her husband "became partners in life." Although he brought 30 years of vending experience to their union, he'd left vending when some family members suggested he become an investor in one of their projects.

"So it really was like we were starting from scratch," says the former human resources manager, who also counts restaurant and fast-food work as part of her background. "But I had three jobs when we met, so he knew I was perfect for this industry because I was already putting in 100 hours per week."

Fun Fact

The National Association of Hosiery Manufacturers places the retail pantyhose industry at $2.8 billion, representing over 1.3 billion pairs of pantyhose, tights, and opaques. No statistics are available for vending's share of the market.

While most food vendors begin with snacks and sodas, Becky P. and her husband formed their Southern California operation as a full-line service. This means they bucked conventional wisdom and offered fresh refrigerated food from the start.

"If you go into cold food with a defeatist attitude, you will be defeated," Becky stresses. Full-line vending is for people who appreciate good food and fine dining. "Don't go into cold food if you're not willing to work it like a restaurant. If you want to work six hours a day or five days a week, forget it."

B.J. S. of Hendersonville, Tennessee, a Nashville suburb, got into vending after owning a construction company in Spain. A native of Sweden, he met his American wife while at school in the United States. The pair lived abroad until 1995, when they moved back to be near her aging parents.

For B.J., owning a vending company was a happenstance. "My father-in-law started the business, and he wanted to retire. I was looking for something to do, so I bought the business from him in July of 1995."

When he took over the business, gross sales just grazed a million per year. Trucks and equipment were antiquated and all the accounting was done by hand. "We bought a lot of trucks," he recalls. "The average age of the fleet was ten years old. We bought ten vehicles in three years, which we financed at a cost of a quarter-million dollars."

Since then, B.J. has tested all the latest technology, beefed up his employee base, and expanded service to cover all five surrounding counties. Gross sales today top $3.5 million.

Pat W. of Preston, Washington, is a retiree. Like B.J. S., her path to vending wasn't direct. Vice president and general manager of a real estate securities and development company, she was downsized in 1990. After taking some time off, she trained to sell insurance.

Four months into her new insurance career, a head-on collision took her out of the work force for three years. In 1994, her daughter heard an ad about telecard vending on a radio program. Although she and her daughter didn't know it at the time, "it was an ad of one of the [less reputable] phone card companies," recounts Pat. "Eventually, it went bankrupt." Although we'll tell more of Pat's story when we discuss vending's dark side in Chapter 3, suffice it to say even her previous corporate experience deciphering the fine print didn't save her from a disastrous start.

By keeping her wits about her and learning quickly from her mistakes, Pat overcame the situation and now runs a telecard operation part time that's exactly the right size. Her income supplements her Social Security, and her time off leaves plenty of time for her grandchildren. She also dabbles in selling antiques on the side.

A Few More Experts

To assist with big-picture issues, you'll also hear from four experts, all with years of experience helping start-up entrepreneurs just like you.

Donald C. Blotner, president of DCB Consulting in Eagan, Minnesota, has been providing management and consulting services to the vending industry since 1985.

His experience includes over 20 years of employment for independently owned vending operations. Prior to founding his consulting firm, Blotner served as the operations manager for a Wisconsin vending business that boasted $3.5 million in annual sales. His responsibilities included redesigning and redefining the roles of key personnel to adapt to changing company and customer needs. Blotner donates considerable time and other resources to assisting new and established operators through NAMA. He presents educational seminars, writes articles for publications, and mentors and volunteers in numerous other capacities.

Vince Gumma is co-owner of American Vending Sales Inc. (AVS) in Chicago. Established in 1971, AVS distributes vending machines, jukeboxes, video games, and pinball and redemption games as well as maintaining an inventory of tens of thousands

---

I'll Buy That

The vending industry breaks down into seven distinct segments. To help you keep score, here are the terms you'll encounter and what each one means.

- ○ *4C's:* an abbreviation that stands for the basics of vending as it evolved (coffee, cup soda, candy, and cigarettes). Today, this segment is most often referred to as "snacks and soda."
- ○ *Full line:* the incorporation of fresh refrigerated items, such as sandwiches and frozen foods, to operators' offerings.
- ○ *OCS:* the commonly used abbreviation for office coffee service, where operators provide equipment and "kits" containing coffee and related items such as sweeteners, creamers, stir sticks, etc. Full-line vending operators often migrate into OCS and vice versa to meet the needs of their clients.
- ○ *Specialty:* refers to a particular line of products, such as french fries, pizza, telecards, and pantyhose, among others
- ○ *Bulk:* the vending of gumballs, toys, stickers, novelties, etc., in loose form. Crossover between full-line and bulk operators in both directions is common but not as frequent as the full-line-OCS connection.
- ○ *Amusements or music/game:* began on the jukebox/pool table side of the business but now includes music machines, video, and arcade games of all sorts. This is another area of crossover with full line, but most often in the form of a separate operation within a larger company due to the specific needs of this market.
- ○ *Street:* most often used to describe mobile operations located in public areas, such as sidewalks and shopping malls. Street vending is generally viewed as a subset or a combination of specialty, full-line, and amusement vending.

▲

Smart Tip

Tip...

To locate industry experts willing to provide you with assistance and advice, contact the National Automatic Merchandising Association or the industry organization for your vending specialty.

of parts. Gumma joined AVS in 1986 after working in the printing ink industry and currently serves as an officer in the Illinois Automatic Merchandising Council (IAMC), a state affiliate of NAMA. He plays an active role in efforts to improve the image of the industry both by assisting with NAMA publicity efforts and helping start-ups understand the realities of owning a vending business. He has received numerous awards from the IAMC and, most recently, the NAMA Chairman's Award for his participation in helping the Illinois vending industry achieve favorable sales tax legislation.

John Ochi is vice president of Five Star Distributors Inc. in Vernon Hills, Illinois. Headquartered in suburban Chicago, the consumables distributor also maintains a location in Atlanta and was purchased by its current owners in 1975. In addition to delivering products, Five Star permits small operators to access its extensive line on a cash-and-carry basis. Ochi began as a warehouse worker in the vending distribution industry in 1974. He came up through the ranks, joining Five Star as partner and vice president in 1994. Serving as a member of vending's front lines from the fast-growth 1970s through the consolidations of the 1990s exposed Ochi to every aspect of the industry. His efforts to improve the industry recently earned Ochi Automatic Merchandising's Distributor of the Year award.

Jim Patterson is principal of Patterson Co. Inc. in Kenilworth, Illinois. The 60-year-old product brokerage firm serves the upper Midwest from its Chicago-area headquarters and is dedicated to matching the right product with the right vending operation. A third-generation member of the family business, Patterson came to the company after finishing college in 1980. Like all our experts, Patterson has experienced both runaway prosperity and the more recent lean years. He brings an affinity for technology as well as an eye for customer service to his active involvement in the improvement of the vending industry, he was recently awarded Automatic Merchandising's Broker of the Year.

Ready, Set, Go

Because no human activity exists in a vacuum, those who prosper in the shark-infested waters we call "The American Way" know it's vital to get out of the trenches and look at the big picture. By arming yourself with the knowledge in this chapter, you, too, have taken an important step toward running a successful business.

Now that you've surveyed the landscape, it's time to learn what you really want to know: How do I start and run a coin-op vending business? To find out, all you have to do is turn the page.

2

A Day in
the Life

Now that you've gotten your feet wet, let's talk about what life as a vending business owner is all about.

First of all, you will get wet feet. And cold feet. And even sweaty feet. This is part of the beauty of vending—every day you spend time outdoors. Although you won't be romping

through your favorite forest, you'll at least get a healthy dose of fresh air and sunshine year-round as you go from place to place.

Rise and Shine

Vending is a flexible business when it comes to daily routine. Many operators run part-time businesses, filling or "servicing" machines during the evenings or on weekends.

Retired Preston, Washington, telecard operator Pat W., services machines three days a week. "Vending is attractive to retirees because it not only supplements your income, but it also keeps your mind active and alert. It's also something a man and a woman can do together or a young family can do. I know a couple that installs Beanie Baby machines. They went into it on a lark, and now they have some serious contracts."

However, if you want to earn a full-time income, traffic becomes a make-or-break proposition. While travel time and distance are important factors to any operator's success, full-timers must adjust their schedules to take advantage of off-peak hours.

In addition, your type of operation will play a part. If you go into cold food, you'll be up before the crack of dawn. "We get up between three and four in the morning," says Northridge, California, full-line operator Becky P., "because we need to be finished servicing machines by 11:30 A.M. for the lunch break."

Making a List

Not surprisingly, your first task of the day is taking stock. Grab your route cards (machine inventory record sheets) and head for your vehicle. Check what you have and decide what you need. Then pull the inventory from storage.

Depending on your type of vending, organize items by location for quick transport from your wheels to your machines. Remember, walking back and forth between your vehicle and your machines is as much wasted time as idling in traffic.

Now load your vehicle, stash your cellular or clip on your pager, and head out.

At a Vendor

Unless you're Jesse "The Body" Ventura, or your inventory is small and light, plan to make at least a couple of trips from vehicle to machine. If you vend them, cold and frozen items go first to minimize the minutes they're not on ice. Pull cold items from the chiller and put them in a cooler. Load your dolly appropriately and head to where your machines await.

When you walk into the break room or wherever your machines are located, first survey the scene. "A footprint on a machine or one that's been pushed back or rocked isn't the sign of a jerk," says Becky P. "It means you should check the coin mechanism and bill changer to see if they're working, and look around for a jam, such as a soda that's hanging up."

Even in the absence of foul play, test the coin and bill mechanisms. Then check and refill the money as needed to ensure your customers get the proper change. If you haven't already done so, remove the footprint and wipe down the front of the machine. As necessary, clean inside as well.

Ready to load? Not yet! Before you put anything in, write down what's been purchased. That's what your route cards are for. (Route cards are also called delivery receipts. See Chapter 13 for an example.) Pay attention to what's hot and what's not. Make notes as necessary to help yourself out later, when you're back at the office.

OK, now load the machine, and move on to the next one.

Bright Idea

In a recent *Vending Times* survey, one entrepreneur reported keeping track of his entire operation with a spreadsheet program on a laptop computer.

Customers Count

Whenever you encounter another person, greet him or her with a smile and a cheery hello. Often, this may occur even before you check your machines.

"I always make the initiative to greet people," asserts Becky P. "The conversation may just be general—how are you, how's the family, the kids, how's work."

While you're servicing, you'll doubtless get special requests. Do everything you possibly can to honor those requests, says Becky. "Right then and there, you've taken a cold inanimate machine and given it a personality," says Becky. "They're going to think of your smiling face when they make that purchase the next time."

And you must honor complaints. "It's very important to listen," she continues. "There have been tons of articles written on this—as long as [the complainer] knows you will handle and respond to a complaint or a problem right away, 98 percent of them will be satisfied and come back. If you blow them off, you've lost that customer."

Who's Who

Every industry has its chain of command and specialized terms to describe the players. To help demystify the vending industry, here's a brief who's who.

- ○ *Broker:* another term for "independent sales representative." Brokers represent manufacturers that are too small or choose not to maintain their own internal sales forces. Although they don't actually sell you products, they're an important source of information and leads for purchasing products at competitive prices.

- ○ *Distributor:* companies that sell equipment and consumables directly to operators. Distributors carry the products of a wide variety of manufacturers.

- ○ *Manufacturer:* a company that produces vending equipment or consumables. Some manufacturers sell to operators directly, but most sell through distributors.

- ○ *Operator:* someone who owns and services vending machines. If you're reading this book, you're interested in becoming an operator. Sometimes the term vendor (see "Learning the Lingo" on page 18) is used to mean operator, but in this book we keep the terms strictly separate.

- ○ *Purchasing cooperative:* an association of operators, usually small businesses, that join together for purchasing purposes. By soliciting distributors as a group, cooperatives assure a certain annual volume and therefore command a lower price.

Upon leaving the room, Becky and her employees also thank everyone who's present. This goes a long way toward building customer loyalty.

Courtesy Calls

Before you move on, pay a visit to the decision maker and perform a ritual similar to the one in the break room. In addition to general inquiries about the person and their family, show an interest in their business situation.

" 'Did you find someone to fill that night position? Do you like the president?'—whatever they're interested in," says Pat W. "I also keep them up on what's going on in the telephone card industry. It makes them feel knowledgeable.

"This is especially true if you present yourself as conservative and reliable," Pat continues, "and you prove it to them consistently."

Trouble Calls

Once you have finished with the machines and humans at your first location, you are off to your next stops. Invariably your cell phone will ring, your pager will buzz, or you will call into your machine and find trouble at the other end of the line.

Finessing trouble calls puts your customer-service, time-management, and problem-solving skills to the test. Each call requires balancing client expectations, revenue loss potential, and the impact on the rest of the route. Whatever you decide, you'll follow up by giving the client your best estimate of when you'll get to the scene of the crime.

When you do arrive at the offending machine, you may find the problem goes beyond a stuck coin. Here's where the quality of your machine manufacturer and distributor comes into play. The better manufacturers offer telephone technical assistance and can navigate you safely through the emergency. If you need a part, a good distributor will quickly have one on its way.

Sales Stops

In between serving machines and fixing jams, you'll also make courtesy calls. Unlike businesses that attract clients through advertising, vending success depends on developing relationships. It also depends on keeping the faith, no matter how long it takes.

 **Beware!**
Never treat a customer's complaint as minor league. "It's not the two-dollar sandwich that you'll lose," Northridge, California, full-line operator Becky P. warns. "It's the fact that they're spending anywhere from one to six dollars a day. If you lose that day in and day out, five, six days a week, what does that add up to at the end of the year?"

"Sales is like playing golf," says Hendersonville, Tennessee, full-line operator B.J. S. "You just keep on doing it. I have one customer I [pitched my service to] for five years and he finally gave in. You have to be stubborn and not take 'No' for an answer. 'No' is for right now; tomorrow the person's mind might change."

Learning the Lingo

You'll find lots of vending lingo explained in the Glossary, but here are the bare-bones terms you need to know to navigate the industry like a pro.

○ *Client.* The person or company who contracts with you to place vendors at their location. A client can also be a customer, but only when he or she is making a purchase from your machine.

○ *Customer.* A person who makes purchases from a vending machine. Often, a customer is an employee at your client's business.

○ *Planogram.* A diagram of an individual vendor with a specific product assigned to each spiral. As vendor capacity grew (most machines now include 40 or more spirals), more sophisticated selection and placement of products (aka merchandising) became necessary for profitability, and planogramming was born.

○ *Route.* The territory covered when servicing machines. The exact definition of this term is indistinct. Sometimes it means the locations you visit in a given day. Sometimes it means the number of people who service locations for your company. For example, if you have 15 machines and you service seven one day and eight another, you'd have two routes. However, you'd also have two routes if you hired an employee and you serviced 50 machines a week and your employee serviced 15 machines a week.

○ *Servicing machines.* The process of cleaning, maintaining, repairing, and, most important, filling vendors. In other words, servicing machines is what you do every day on a route.

○ *Spiral.* The space allotted for a type of product in a food vendor. Because snack machines move products forward via a metal spiral mechanism, the term has been adopted to mean any individual offering, snack, sandwich, soda, etc. However use of the term varies within the industry. For example, in a telecard machine, a spiral is called a bin.

○ *Vendor.* The abbreviated term for "vending machine." In the industry, vendor sometimes means operator, but in this book we keep the two terms strictly separate.

Back at the Office

When you finish your route and return to the office, your day's not done. The load of coins and wad of bills requires counting, sorting, and logging in your bookkeeping system.

Sound boring? You would not be the first person to think so. "Don't fall into the trap of thinking, 'Oh, wow, look at all this money I have' and going out and buying a Corvette," says Becky P. "You have to be very, very disciplined in a cash business because, at the end of the month, you have your equipment loans, insurance payments, merchandise invoices, rent, gasoline bills, and sales taxes. Vending is a real business—you have to take care of your bookwork. You have to know where you are."

After you've finished with your paperwork, your other chores include merchandising, marketing, ordering, and various other administrative duties.

For example, you may have noticed out on the route that tortilla chips are hot at Location A, but at Location B you can't keep enough microwave popcorn in stock. In retail, proper merchandising translates directly to profits, so you take out your planograms (diagrams of where merchandise goes in your machines) for each location and figure out an arrangement that boosts space for the movers without impacting other strong sellers. You may study your bookwork and realize a location is no longer profitable. Then you'll need to make a plan: Do you pull out immediately or try some other strategies?

When you're through with merchandising, turn to marketing. Return inquiry calls and initiate some of your own.

In Tomorrow's Life

For some types of products, your next step is packaging. "I buy hose in bulk and repackage it into small boxes," says Baltimore pantyhose operator Janice M.

With telecards, it's time to place your orders. "I make sure I have a five-day lead when I make an order," Pat W. remarks. "And that's because I keep a tight watch on my inventory. [Unless you have a lot of money to tie up in inventory,] you're best off if you keep your office inventory as low as possible."

Food operators use this time to stock up. "Those who start out without much working capital literally make collections during the day and [use the funds] to buy their product that night for the next day," Becky P. notes. "If you're big enough, or have space to warehouse products, then you can have things delivered and reload with items you have in stock."

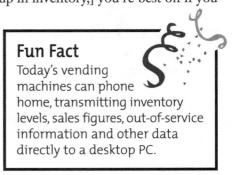

Fun Fact
Today's vending machines can phone home, transmitting inventory levels, sales figures, out-of-service information and other data directly to a desktop PC.

▲

Dump Your Cash

Keeping mounds of coins around is more than a temptation for your ten-year-old; it's an open invitation for more serious predators. Always take deposits to your financial institution straight away.

A Spoonful of Motivation

Although you'll certainly bring a variety of skills to the table, here are a few personality traits you definitely should have.

○ *Cash-wise.* Because you receive cash immediately rather than billing your customers and receiving payment later, attention to basic bookkeeping is a must. "If you can't balance a checkbook, don't get into this business," stresses consumables distributor John Ochi of Five Star Distributors in Vernon Hills, Illinois. "Fifteen to 20 percent of the operators who purchase from us are bankrupt, but they don't know it yet. Just because you have cash flow doesn't mean you're profitable."

○ *Organized.* Gone are the days of servicing machines without a plan. Today, convenience stores, company cafes, and telecommuting all contribute to fierce competition for vending dollars. "Proper route structuring and merchandising are key," emphasizes Donald Blotner of Eagan, Minnesota-based DCB Consulting. "You can't just take on a location because it's offered. You must take travel and sales potential into account. And you must monitor every location closely to ensure every spiral is turning over swiftly enough."

○ *Gregarious.* Vending may seem like the perfect occupation for an introvert—it's all about inanimate objects and inanimate machines, right? Wrong! "Vending is relationship-based," says Blotner. "Most of your business will come from referrals. Therefore, your customers, clients, and suppliers must think highly of your business. Building a significant reservoir of goodwill takes a warm person who's not only willing to give 110 percent, but offers without being asked—and does it with a smile."

○ *Self-motivated.* Although the need for this trait practically goes without saying, the amount of literature on the topic belies its mystery. "People don't realize how hard we work," says Northridge, California, operator Becky P. "Vending's not much different than running a restaurant—it's evenings, it's holidays, it's Saturdays and Sundays. You have to be passionate and you have to love it."

Before you do, ask your bank how they want you to present your dough. "Banks are particular," says Pat W. "They like to have the money bundled in a certain way. You may be bringing in several thousand dollars at a time, and they have to count it."

What's My Take?

What you make in vending depends on how many machines you service. "A lot of people will buy three machines and fill them on the weekend and be happy as a clam," Pat W. explains. "It makes them $500 extra a month, which they can use for a down payment on a car, Christmas gifts, or to save for their kids to go to college. For myself, I would like to grow my business."

No matter what your business' size, ex-pect your nets to be low. "When it's all said and done, if I keep one half to two cents for every dollar we make, I'm lucky," stresses Becky P. "The pie-in-the-skies give everybody the impression that you put all that money [you collect from a machine] in your pocket. But if you're legitimate, no ma'am. Vending's like every other retail business—[on average] you get to keep about a penny, so you have to work on volume."

Although all our experts stressed vending requires hard work for relatively small per-machine profits, they also emphasize that those who do it right are prosperous. If what we've said in these first two chapters leaves you cold, maybe it's time to consider a different industry. On the other hand, perhaps you're pumped because your skills fit the profile. If so, read on and we'll tell you exactly what you need to know.

Tip...

Smart Tip
Small operators who don't employ an armored carrier service say they deter theft by taking cash to the bank at irregular times rather than the same time every day.

Start from Scratch or Buy a Business

Everything you need to build a vending operation from the ground up is right in front of you. But for whatever reason, you may be wondering if there's a way to jump-start the process.

▲

Indeed, there is. There are also hundreds of individuals who fall victim to vending business opportunity scams every year. To avoid being one of them, read this chapter, which presents some valuable dos and don'ts.

One Operator's Story

So pervasive is the business opportunity scam in vending that the industry has its own term for the scam: Blue Sky. Although we learned much about Blue Skies from everyone we spoke to, the best way to tell you about them is through one operator's story.

After a financially draining three-year recovery from a head-on collision, Pat W. of Preston, Washington, needed income. Her daughter, who lived in Virginia, heard an ad for selling telecards and called her mother with the idea. "It was 1994, and my daughter told me phone cards were big on the East Coast," Pat recalls. "I did not even know what one was. She gave me the 800 number, and I called the company, which sold vending machines as well as phone cards."

"For about three or four months I talked to an awful lot of people many times," she continues. "These were people who were referred to me by the company as people who were buying cards from them and had been successful. I also went out to stores around here to see who was and wasn't handling phone cards, what they cost, and to see what kind of money the merchant was getting from suppliers."

Because the industry was so new, Pat's research turned up as many questions as answers. "I would go in to a merchant and ask, 'Do you carry phone cards?' and they'd say, 'What are those?' I'd talk to my friends and say, 'What do you know about phone cards?' and they'd say, 'Never heard of 'em. What are they?' "

Undaunted, she continued her research. "I read all the info that was sent to me by this company. They're located in Florida, and the state of Florida required a full disclosure booklet. I was used to reading the fine print, so I read the booklet. I was also looking for magazines that might be advertising for other phone card companies. But I could not find any."

Eventually, Pat located a phone card distributor in her state. "He said, 'I can give you a certain percentage discount if you buy $100,000 worth of cards.' Well, I didn't talk to him very long. I wasn't in that class.

"And I was frightened—I didn't have very much money after three years of no income," she admits. "I had pretty well come on hard times and needed income pretty badly. But the results of that accident left me unable to

Fun Fact

Blue Skies are so prevalent in the industry that the Federal Trade Commission devotes an entire brochure to vending scams. To obtain *Business Opportunities: Avoiding Vending Machine and Display Rack Scams,* call (877) 382-4357.

stand behind a counter and unable to sit behind a desk. I was in bad shape."

Finally, Pat took the plunge. "It cost $5,100 for the machine, cards, and location. The machine was not full of cards, it just had a certain number of cards that came with it, which was $1,000 retail. The location was in a gas station/deli within 30 miles of my home."

Not long afterward she learned the truth. "Today the machines are worth about $1,400 brand new, with a base. The standard cost for a location is $300 in the industry. At that time, you could purchase $1,000 worth of cards for a 40 percent discount, which means they cost $600. So that's $4,100 that you're paying for a

> **Beware!**
> Advertisements promising big bucks for part-time or minimal work are scam-alerts. "You can't just put the machines out there and sit on the couch," Preston, Washington, telecard operator Pat W. warns. "It doesn't work that way. You always have to work for your meal ticket, no matter what business you're in."

machine that costs something like $1,400. It was a real rip-off." To make matters worse, the company wasn't even a manufacturer, as Pat had been led to believe. "They never handled the machines. They just brokered them. They just called the manufacturer, and the machines were sent to the buyer.

"Eventually, that company was prohibited from selling machines anymore because the whole thing was a scam," she concludes. "The FCC stepped in and kept them from selling anymore, and the FBI walked in too. Finally, they went bankrupt."

Who Can I Trust?

Fortunately, this tragic tale has a happy ending and, as you know, Pat is a prosperous vending operator today. But it does beg the question "Who can you trust?"

The answer is many people. First of all, you should always check with the attorney general's office both in the state where you live and the state where the company you're considering doing business with is located. Then there's the Federal Trade Commission and The National Fraud Information Center to call on for help and information. Next, turn to industry associations. For vending that's NAMA, but there may be other helpful organizations (such as the International Telecard Association, in the case of prepaid phone cards). If industry associations haven't heard of the company in question, be wary. Even if the company is not a member of the association, the organization probably knows about them if they're legitimate.

Another good resource is the library. Ask librarians to help you search business databases to locate the outfit in question. Red flags are failure to turn up or being in a different business than they stated, such as Pat's experience where the company didn't actually make the machines.

▲

You can also call the offices of industry publications *Automatic Merchandiser* and *Vending Times*. Both magazines produce annual listings of everyone in the business. Even in a new business, such as telecards, they'll know some manufacturers to call who can give you advice.

Finally, ask industry associations to put you in touch with veteran vendors outside your area of competition. As we mentioned in the first chapter, many operators dabble

---

Anatomy of a Blue Sky

Here are a few basic tips on spotting a Blue Sky opportunity, drawn from the FTC publication *Business Opportunities: Avoiding Vending Machine and Display Rack Scams* and the book *Vending for Investors*, both of which are listed in the Appendix.

○ Call the secretary of state and attorney general of the state where the company is located. Determine how long they've been in business and any business aliases; find out who the principal owners are and whether any complaints have been filed against them.

○ Ask for substantiation in writing, particularly on income. Look for calculations that include all the expense categories shown in Chapter 15.

○ Visit the locations and anticipated locations promised by the locator. Ask the owner or manager about traffic, buying patterns, competition, etc.

○ Avoid any opportunity that claims there's no selling involved in the operation of a vending business.

○ Contact the marketing department of any company whose brand names are used in advertisements. Determine if they're actually sponsoring or backing the outfit in question.

○ Comparison shop, just like you would for any other item.

○ Avoid trusting references provided by the company unless you have absolute proof they're not a friend, employee, or shill hired for the job.

○ Ask industry associations and the advertising departments of industry publications about the company.

○ Talk with those already in the business. Find such individuals through industry associations.

○ Set aside your pride. Assuming you're too smart to be conned is a common mistake.

○ Persevere until you find the right opportunity. If you learn from others' mistakes, you'll soon be on your way to an exciting new career.

---

in more than one vending category, and they're a reservoir of information waiting to be tapped.

Know the Purpose

One of the best ways to avoid a scam is to take a moment to sit back and assess. "I've helped people get started in the vending business," notes 20-year veteran Wayne D., who has also provided countless operators with counsel and advice. "I think it's important to understand what your business is about before you get into it," says the full-line operator in Burnsville, Minnesota.

"What are your objectives?" he asks. "Is it to be in business on your own or to get rich? Vending's not a get-rich-quick business. Like any other retail business, it's a long, drawn-out process. I'm only 55, but I've just watched people flounder. People tell me, 'I want to work less and be my own boss.' But don't plan on working less. My wife and I worked nights and Saturdays and Sundays when we started.

"For eight years I didn't take a dime out of the business," continues Wayne. "Go get a part-time job for 20 to 30 hours a week [in addition to your full-time employment] and see what it's like," he suggests. "Then think about what it's like without taking any money out of it. If you have a decent job, chances are you're going to make more money in the first few years than in the vending business."

Reputable Opportunities

Although we've painted a scary picture, don't reject the vending industry, a business opportunity, or a franchise out of hand. There are plenty of reputable companies to help you get started. Your job is separating the wheat from the chaff.

Fortunately, vending is a close-knit industry. While there are a lot of very small operators who don't participate in associations like NAMA, most everyone who hires an employee gets into the loop. And because they've all been where you are, you'll quickly find out how happy they are to lend newcomers a hand.

Even equipment distributors urge newcomers to call upfront. "Honestly, I get people on the phone in tears," says Vince Gumma of Chicago's American Vending Sales. "They've already spent $40,000 or $50,000 in retirement savings, and I can't help them."

Again, the key is to network before you buy. Regardless whether your specialty is new or old, vending trade magazines, NAMA, and veterans like those interviewed in this book offer a big-picture vantage point they're eager to share. Take advantage of their knowledge and experience.

Smart Tip

Tip...

Veteran operators often mentor newbies whose market areas are outside their own. To get connected, contact the industry association for the vending specialty you're considering.

4

Finding
Your Niche

While not as glamorous as, say, becoming a jungle guide, the life of a vending operator sounds perfect to you. Knowing this much means your cup is half full. Topping it off requires determining what type of vending you'd like to do and whether there's a demand for you to supply.

▲

The business lingo for these activities is targeting your market and conducting market research. Think of these steps as akin to feeding yourself— you have to know what kind food you like and where to find it. The more you know, the more satisfied you are. Similarly, the more thorough your research, the more satisfied (profitable) your business is.

> To narrow your vending options, first decide whether you're a trailblazer or path follower.

Do some business owners skip or shortchange the process of evaluating their market's potential? You bet. But they're the ones who flounder or fail.

Since you're reading this book to succeed, use the handy tools provided in this chapter for your upfront work, and come back to it for guidance as your business grows.

To narrow your vending options, first decide whether you're a trailblazer or path follower. Trailblazers enter new markets, such as telecards, or define their own market, like pantyhose. Path followers prefer tried-and-true markets such as snacks and soda. Which one should you choose? Either is completely appropriate, and both have their pluses and minuses.

Where No One's Gone Before

The main advantages to trailblazing are obvious: There's little or no competition and lots of room for growth. This means you're first in line rather than just another voice in the crowd. And you won't be looking over your shoulder as much because there are plenty of clients to go around.

The principal downside is lack of familiarity and support. Not only must you convince a prospect your company is best for the job; you have to sell them on the concept as well. And there's less of a network for you to lean on for information and advice.

"A lot of people don't want to hear about something new," says Baltimore pantyhose vending innovator Janice M. "The attitude is 'I don't care; go away' unless you've been around for 30 years and they recognize the name." In addition, corporate procurement officers are often men, and they simply don't understand the challenges faced by pantyhose wearers. "Then when they get [a machine], they find out it's something they actually like."

In Pat W.'s case, the initial difficulty was determining whether or not telecards were profitable and what a reasonable price for a machine was. "There wasn't very much out there about phone cards," says the Preston, Washington, telecard operator. "The industry was still in its infancy, and a prepaid phone card was almost unheard of in Washington state."

Familiar Turf

Not surprisingly, the flip side of trailblazing is path following. Advice, information, and support abound. "If I were starting up, I'd contact the local or state chapter of NAMA and ask for references outside of my marketplace," says Wayne D., the full-line operator in Burnsville, Minnesota. "Most of us aren't too hung up about competitors. We would rather help new operators so they don't add to the stigma that vending machines never work."

The downside to so much support is, of course, competition. But it's not an insurmountable obstacle. The key is showing prospects you are head and shoulders above the rest. Economic, demographic, and technological changes offer entrepreneurs opportunities for success, even in today's crowded market.

For example, Pat W. stocks telecards with lower rates to Russia in her vendors at a convenience store near a naval base where Russians come ashore. "One of the big tricks is to get a good discount for the market you're in, so you have to know your market and stock the right cards. Then, the merchant knows the people who want those cards are going to come back to buy cards and maybe even a few more things."

An increasing concentration of Latinos in her town led Becky P., a Northridge, California, full-line operator, to develop another unique approach. In addition to stocking appropriate food items, she also conducts educational sessions for non-English speakers.

Stay in the Zone

Although trailblazing vs. path following is a philosophical dilemma, the recommended size of your market area is not. Since drive time and fuel costs are significant factors, it's wise to stay within a 30-mile radius of your office, 50 at most. This constraint alone may help determine your vending type. For example, if you live in a rural area that's already served by a local food vending operation, a nonfood operation might be a more viable choice. On the other hand, if the headquarters of the existing food operator is miles away, you may be able to offer a more cost-effective option.

Smart Tip

Tip...

Defining the limits of your start-up zone is as easy as 1-2-3. Take a piece of string or thread and measure out 30 miles using your map's "scale of miles." Place one end of the string at your location and a pencil at the other. Draw a circle with your location as the center. Voilà!

▲

Know Thy Options

We've already discussed which vending markets are currently the largest, but the success of pioneering entrepreneurs like Janice M. and Pat W. shows it's wise to look at the forest before focusing on a tree.

To find out about the many types of vending machines and products already available, check out the annual buyer's guides produced by *Automatic Merchandiser* and *Vending Times*. While there's plenty of overlap between the two, not all options appear in each publication. If your library doesn't subscribe, call the publications directly using the contact information in the Appendix.

Go with Your Strengths

The best vending specialty for you may not become clear until you've done some market research. As you mull over the options, remember nobody's perfect. Always ask yourself whether a given idea plays to your strengths. For example, a new specialty may require teaching skills and the patience of a saint. "For the first couple of years, I taught every client how to use phone cards because they didn't know how," Pat W. comments.

Even established vending formats offer challenges. Let's say you're interested in snacks and soda, and the two-year colleges are underserved in your market. As we showed you in Chapter 2, interacting with customers is important to your success. If talking to young people with brightly colored hair and pierced tongues turns you off, bypass this opportunity, no matter how golden.

Mission: Possible

A mission statement tells the world what your company is about. It generally also includes something about your goals and, sometimes, how you intend to achieve them. Writing a mission statement is a vital part of finding your niche because it helps you define your target market and stay focused on what's important. Use the "Mission Statement Worksheet" on page 33 and the examples below to come up with your own.

Although in many industries a long, detailed mission is de rigueur, vending operators generally prefer something succinct. Here are three real-life examples:

1. "To provide the highest-quality vending service in Nashville."
2. "Quality through integrity. To provide the very best customer satisfaction."
3. "To be a cut above. Good enough isn't enough; it has to be perfect."

Mission Statement Worksheet

Use this worksheet to brainstorm a mission statement for your business. The components of a mission statement include:

- ○ *Future goals:* your vision of your company in a year, five years, and beyond
- ○ *Client perceptions:* your vision of how you want your clients to think of you
- ○ *Industry perceptions:* your vision of how you want the vending industry to think of you

Mission Statement for: _____(your business name)

_____

_____

_____

_____

_____

_____

_____

_____

_____

_____

_____

_____

_____

_____

_____

Fun Fact

The Census Bureau reports that between 1995 and 2025 most foreign immigrants will settle in the Northeast and the West. During the same period, most of the South's population increase will be due to inter-state migrants from the Northeast and Midwest.

Assessing Your Economy

As you narrow the specialty options, include an economic assessment as part of your market research. For example, vending Tex-Mex is absurd if your local ethnic population is Hmong. Nor will targeting factories work if they're all headed south. Instead, cater to Hmong food tastes or target hospitals instead of factories. In general, look for areas of growth or market segmentation, such as a rising population of women aged 24 to 30.

"I look for businesses that have upscale clienteles," Janice M. explains. "Lawyers, accountants, senators, etc., because their secretaries and assistants are always going to be professional-looking. So I know there's a market there for me."

Except in the most depressed areas, a new niche or angle can almost always be found.

Evaluate an Innovation

If you're considering a vending specialty that's your own brainchild, or even one that's relatively new, conduct some direct consumer surveys. Surveys can be informal oral inquiries, formal written questionnaires, or a combination of both.

"One day, we were doing presentations [during a Women Entrepreneurs of Baltimore class I was attending], and I started talking to a few of the women," Janice M. recalls. "I asked them how they would feel if they could purchase pantyhose through a vending machine. Everybody said, 'That's really cool. Who do you know that's doing that?' And I said *me*. They all looked at me and said, 'That is great. Yeah, I'd purchase them. I cannot tell you how many times I have been to a wedding or a funeral or job interview or church on Sunday when everything is closed—that would be great.' "

Spurred on by the enthusiastic response, Janice developed a written survey. "I actually have footage of me walking down the street with a clipboard asking people what they thought: Would you buy pantyhose from a vending machine? If you wouldn't, why not? I actually liked [this method] better than anything else because you're dealing with live people who are telling you right there what they really think. They didn't know me from Eve, so they didn't have any reason to sugarcoat anything. People are brutally honest when you're doing research, which is fine because it helps."

Due to the success of her efforts, Janice continues to rely on them. "I still have that [survey] on file because I'm going to use it again. In fact, I used it when I went out to

Baltimore/Washington International Airport because they didn't see the need [for pantyhose vending]. So I told them about the survey and all the women who'd checked 'yes' beside 'Would you purchase this from a vending machine?' Then my contact said, 'Send me a package.' " Turn to page 36 to see Janice's "Market Research Survey." You can tailor it to your own specific vending niche.

Site Surveys

For traditional vending specialties, spend time surveying your operating radius from the ground. Take a few exploratory road trips and observe the mix of businesses, schools, hospitals, and high-rises. Even if you've lived in the area your whole life, you'll see things differently when you are looking at it with an entrepreneur's eye.

Stop in at potential locations and see what's already vended there. Is there room for more variety or a more targeted product mix? Are the machines clean and well maintained? Are they new and attractive or old and shabby?

Follow Janice's lead and survey people using the machines. What do they think of the service and product mix? What would they like more or less of? Are they generally satisfied or dissatisfied? Why? Listen carefully and take good notes. Know you have found an opportunity wherever there are signs of an operator who's doing things "the way they've always been done" rather than keeping pace with the times.

Looks Can Deceive

If you come to a site that seems right but there's no vending in sight, don't conclude you've stumbled on the perfect niche. The location may be too small, too close to other options, or affected by some other factor.

Traditionally, companies with fewer than 50 employees haven't been profitable for operators. "Most of the people who come into our facility think they've found a niche market in small locations," notes machine distributor Vince Gumma of Chicago's American Vending Sales. "If there isn't a machine in that location today, then there's probably a reason."

Ferreting out that reason can sometimes be a challenge, but talking to the office or building manager is a good place to start. Most likely, the problem has been cookie-cutter vending. If so, collect enough demographic, wage, and related information to determine whether the location offers profitability if you customize.

> **Fun Fact**
> A recent survey published in *Automatic Merchandiser* found only 21.5 percent of operators pursue small accounts, leaving room for the entrepreneur who's willing to customize, improvise, and innovate.

▲

Market Research Survey

Dear Consumer,

We need your help. Please tell us how we can better improve our services and products for you.

1. Would you purchase pantyhose from a vending machine if available at your location? Why or why not? _____

_____

_____

2. What price would you expect to pay for them? _____

_____

_____

3. What colors would you choose (white, black, gray, navy, etc.)? What sizes (small, medium, tall, full-figure, etc.)? _____

_____

_____

4. Would you purchase products from our catalog through the mail? Why or why not? _____

_____

_____

_____

5. What age range are you in? 18-24, 24-36, 36-45, 45 and up? _____

_____

Any additional comments: _____

_____

_____

We would like to take this time to say thank you.

For a free sample of our products, please send your request to:

A-1 Vending Machines
P.O. Box 0101
Baltimore, MD 21205
Or call us at: (123) 456-7890

Source: McLean Machines & Co. Inc.

Pick Up the Phone

Although it's important to do some driving around, surveying by telephone is more cost-effective. "Obviously, you can cover a lot more over the phone," says B.J. S., the full-line vendor from Hendersonville, Tennessee. "I called Dun & Bradstreet and bought a database listing all Nashville companies including contact names and phone numbers. It cost $100 and came on diskette, so it was easy to break down and sort."

Once you've identified prospects to call, create a survey like the "Location Evaluation" form on page 143 in Chapter 11. Customize it to your area by adding questions based on the results of your economic assessment, remembering to include inquiries that measure the quality of existing vending as well as quantity and type.

More Competition Than You Think

New vending operators often define their competition only in terms of other vending businesses. However, this assumption is far too narrow.

"We are a retail business," emphasizes John Ochi of Five Star Distributors in Vernon Hills, Illinois. "The machines are a form of retailing; there just isn't a human being sitting inside the box handing the stuff out."

This means any retailer who carries similar products is vying for your customer's dollars. "Too many operators think they have a captive audience," observes 20-year vending veteran Wayne D., a full-line operator in Burnsville, Minnesota. "But you don't. I like to say the only captive audience we have is the women's prison."

Another hindrance to vending is that you're competing against a stigma that's firmly entrenched. "The biggest problem the vending industry has is there's a public perception that it's the last resort," Ochi asserts. "Everybody's had bad experiences buying through a vending machine because some operator didn't make sure the machine gave good service."

The moral of the story: When you're conducting market research, look around the neighborhood for other retail options. If you're going into food, ask how long lunch hours last and if employees generally leave the premises. Include a visual or qualitative survey of potential locations to determine attitudes toward the current operator.

Above all, remember that once you hang out your shingle, the spotlight will shine on you just as hard as you're shining it on others. Be prepared to go the extra mile, and your business will thrive.

▲

Bulldozer Chasing

Those lucky enough to live where office or industrial buildings seemingly inflate overnight have one of the best markets around.

"Whenever a new building would go up we'd literally drive around and count cars in the parking lot," says Becky P. of her tactics during start-up. "Then we'd go back at night to see who had night shifts because those employees are a captive audience."

Partnering with a Player

In food vending, the fight for market share for midrange companies is particularly fierce. As proud and independent as any start-up, owners of vending businesses of this size are either finding new efficiencies or giving in to mergers with a competitor.

> ## Bright Idea
> Consult the annual National Automatic Merchandising Association (NAMA) directory to identify larger operators in your area, but don't approach these larger operators with the partnering concept. Instead, conduct research or ask for advice. People like to be helpful, and you'll still plant the right seed in your interviewee's head.

This pressure-cooker environment is offering start-ups a new opportunity, according to John Ochi of Vernon Hills, Illinois-based Five Star Distributors. "An operator could have a stop today that has 150 workers and tomorrow it could have 20. The operator that sold services to this client based on a population of 150 has a completely different perspective when the population drops to 20. They may be looking for someone to partner with because they may not want to do anything with fewer than 50 people."

"I know a couple of guys in the area who partnered with larger operators," Ochi says. "And they've been successful because they found the right guy to partner with."

Starting from Endings

Yet another area to research is operators who are hanging up their gloves. "In your cash & carries, you'll often see fliers for people going out of business," notes Becky P.

If you purchase another company, expect to pay 30 to 40 percent of the operation's gross sales, says Donald Blotner of DCB Consulting in Eagan, Minnesota. "Given the costs, such as interest expense on equipment loans, if you have the available cash, skip start-up, and capitalize on an established operation."

Bullets to Dodge

By purchasing his business from his retiring father-in-law, B.J. S. did just that. However, he stresses caution. "Look at the equipment—not so much age as the appearance. If it's clean and old, then someone's taken care of it. You can see pretty quickly if the equipment's been abused or it's been refurbished or whatever."

Dollar Stretcher

If you need legal advice and are a National Automatic Merchandising Association member, you're eligible for assistance at a discounted rate.

In addition, B.J. emphatically recommends retaining a knowledgeable attorney to steer you through the process. "Unfortunately, in this industry, I think the income statement only tells part of the truth," he warns. "Ask the owner upfront how much he's skimming off the top. At $1 million in sales and below, I'd say 90 to 99 percent of operators would not run a straight book.

"As a prudent businessperson, I wouldn't take somebody's word for it," B.J. continues. "Make up some type of contract where you have a safeguard. Put the excess in escrow or allow for a 10 percent fluctuation or whatever it is. You'll see in the first week if [the income statement is accurate]. But you're not going to see it until you own it."

Build It Slowly

Once you've completed your market research, keep it handy. The data you gather is as useful for sales leads as it is for diagnosis. And it can even help you evaluate the viability of routes that become available as you begin to grow.

The year after he started, Wayne D. and his wife began following just such a strategy. "In 1979, we bought another small route that was a spin-off of a larger vending company's routes. We worked out a plan of what we were trying to accomplish so that we'd build [the operation] up to where I could leave R.J. Reynolds." It took another five years, but Wayne stayed focused and eventually reached his goal.

5

Structural
Strategies

You've done your homework. You know your mission. You're ready to hang out your shingle.

Whoa! What'll you put on that shingle? Who needs to be notified? And what exactly do they want to know?

▲

What's Your M.O.?

By this point you probably know if you're going it alone or bringing others on board. Either way, local, state, and federal agencies, including the omnipresent IRS, want to know your modus operandi: Are you a sole proprietorship, partnership, or corporation?

Most vending operators stick with the least complicated version, the sole proprietorship. Even spousal teams, pervasive in the industry, usually select this option.

Despite the fact that her husband brought all the vending experience to their relationship, on paper it's Northridge, California, Becky P.'s business. "When we started, it was highly beneficial to be a woman or minority business owner because it opened accounts to us." Financing also came easier, says Becky, due to programs targeting women and minority business owners.

Incorporating is another popular choice for vending entrepreneurs. "With a corporation, there's more of a wall between me and my personal assets," asserts Preston, Washington, telecard operator Pat W. "My machines are difficult to move because I add 300-pound weights to each one as well as bolting them to the floor. If a little kid is fooling around in a laundromat while his mom is focusing on her laundry, and he pulls one of my machines over and breaks his leg, his mom is going to sue me." Being incorporated protects Pat personally.

B.J. S., the Hendersonville, Tennessee, entrepreneur who became an operator by purchasing his father-in-law's vending business, echoes Pat's logic. "When you're incorporated, the corporation carries the liability instead of you personally. You can also use it when negotiating with banks by reminding them the corporation guarantees the note. Even though the bank will probably still ask you for a personal guarantee, you can use your corporate status during negotiations."

As for partnerships, operators who attempted this option urge caution. "In vending, a partnership is a marriage getting ready to fail," says Burnsville, Minnesota, full-line operator Wayne D., who experimented with forming nonfamily partnerships early on. The three- to five-year ramp-up most vending start-ups require is what makes partnerships a difficult choice. "Over the course of time, people's ambitions change. Generally, the entrepreneur's motivations and skills far outweigh those of the people he takes in for the partnership."

A Name of Your Own

Once you've committed to a structure, it's time to give your enterprise a name.

If you consult the Yellow Pages, you'll quickly discover many vending company names are simply variations on their owner's names, such as "A.J. Vending" for "Al Jones." While a similar title for your firm is perfectly acceptable, today's fiercely competitive vending industry demands an identity with an edge.

One of the operators we interviewed wanted her customers to know she viewed them as unique individuals with sophisticated palates, not automatons chewing cut-rate cud. "I didn't want Joe Blow Vending or XYZ Vending," the entrepreneur says of her business name, A Matter of Taste. "I wanted something that gave my business meaning. So I got my thesaurus out and started putting words together. [I decided] A Matter of Taste is [like] life—it's very much a matter of taste because what one person loves, another person cannot stand. Over the years, we've gotten great response to our name; people really like it."

While her creative process was less complex, another of our entrepreneurs knew she needed a memorable name to introduce herself and her concept. "I thought, well, it's a vending machine, how about McLean Machines? I started to like it and everyone I talked to about it said, 'You know, that's a catchy little name.' "

Those who purchase an existing operation should let the company's current standing be their guide. If your acquisition has had difficulty meeting expectations, use a new designation to signal a fresh start. On the other hand, monikers with positive associations should be retained. Even though Van Vending isn't exactly bedazzling, one of our operators acknowledges retaining it "because it had a good reputation."

To start your own list of name possibilities, jot down some simple ideas such as those based on your region's name (example: New Mexico Vending). As the roster

The Name Game

Although the Internet is hot, surfing your Yellow Pages for name ideas can be just as effective. Browsing the vending category will give you an idea of what's already spoken for.

Vending operators emphasize that being successful means viewing your business as retail sales delivered by a machine. So flip to the retail sections that correspond with your business, and see what strikes your fancy. For example, if you're going into food, turn to restaurants, and notice which names make your mouth water. Then, consider a variation such as transforming Prime Steakhouse into Prime Vending Services.

Scribble down several options in case you discover the one you want is already taken. Check the business White Pages as well as the Yellow Pages, and note other businesses with the same or similar names. This will save you time, effort, and even disappointment when you register your business name. Although your state may allow you to use the same name as another business, give your enterprise a head start by choosing a moniker that stands out from the crowd.

Name Brainstorming Worksheet

List three ideas based on the type of vending you plan to provide (e.g., food, tele-cards, personal products):

1. _____

2. _____

3. _____

List three ideas based on descriptive adjectives (e.g., speedy, zesty, reliable):

1. _____

2. _____

3. _____

List three ideas based on your geographic location (e.g., neighborhood, county, region):

1. _____

2. _____

3. _____

List three ideas based on a well-known local feature (e.g., terrain, historical reference, native plants or animals):

1. _____

2. _____

3. _____

❑ Check your local White Pages and Yellow Pages for businesses with the same or similar names. A similar name is out if it's in the same industry (Yellow Pages) and less effective if there are a number of them across industries (White Pages).

❑ Contact your local business name authority to see if your favorite names are available.

❑ Try your favorite out loud and over the phone to make sure it's easy to pronounce and understand. Get feedback from family, friends, and others, such as contacts within the industry.

It's a go? Excellent! Now register it and make it your own.

grows, try out your favorites on friends and relatives—in person, but especially over the phone. Call your guinea pigs, and ask them to phone you back. Then, answer with your new name. What was the caller's impression of the name? Can they correctly repeat it? Remember, for the average person, phone comprehension is atrocious. No matter how clearly you enunciate, a name like A&J Vending will always sound like "ANJ Vending."

Although your name should be a reflection of you, jump-start your brainstorming by checking out the names of successful vending operators in the Appendix of this book. Then use the "Name Brainstorming Worksheet" at left to narrow down your choices.

Make It Official

With your favored moniker option in hand, it's time to get it in writing. Basically, this means contacting the appropriate government entity, checking to see if the name is available, and registering the name as your own, generally for a fee. Don't be alarmed by the terms "fictitious" or "assumed." This simply means the name you're using to do business.

Depending on the state you live in, you may or may not be allowed to use a name someone else registered first. In some states, such as Iowa, you may not even be required to register at all.

Regardless of the law, registering now prevents misery later. Why? Because the longer you're in business, the more valuable your good name will be to you. If you've registered it, there are no worries when a squatter comes along. If you haven't registered, even the best (read: most expensive) attorney may not charm the court.

In addition, financial institutions in some states require proof of business name registration before opening a simple business checking account. Because the IRS insists on separate personal and business accounts, save yourself some time by registering your business name before going to the bank.

In states where you're required to register, you'll likely find a variation on Minnesota's: Call the Secretary of State's office and request the appropriate forms. Before you hang up, you may ask the status of three name options. If one of them is available, you fill out the forms when they arrive, and mail them back with your registration fee. If none of the names are available, call back with another three options until you find a winner.

Smart Tip

Consider the future when you're selecting a business name. Avoid names that prevent expansion into other vending lines such as "Smith's Soda Services." And if you're a woman, no matter how committed you are to your current identity, it's wise to remember your last name is subject to change.

> **Bright Idea**
>
> Although not required, sole proprietors without employees may obtain a Federal Employer Identification Number. Applying for and using this number on your tax returns and all official documents (such as business checking accounts and contracts with clients) is an excellent way to differentiate you and your business in the eyes of the IRS.

One way to speed this process is by using the fax-back or Internet services many state governments now offer for obtaining forms and checking name availability. Using these services reduces the time it takes to lock in your favored business name. If you are not connected, most public libraries offer Internet access, and any business you patronize regularly can be tapped to receive a fax on your behalf.

After your name registration forms are processed, you'll receive an official certificate in the mail. Then you have a specified period of time during which you must advertise your business name in a local newspaper and document the ad to the state. If you don't take out an ad immediately, you'll likely be contacted by a company that places such ads and provides the necessary paperwork to the government, for a nominal fee.

Framing your dba (doing business as) certificate and hanging it on the wall is a nice way to make your new business seem more real, especially if you're like most vending start-ups and operate out of a home office.

Homebased Zone

Speaking of home offices, your next encounter with the government should be your local zoning authority. Although the tradition of homebased businesses is older than the Liberty Bell, residential neighborhoods value child-friendly streets, prompting municipalities to restrict business activities accordingly.

Generally, residential zoning regulations ban enterprises that generate considerable customer and employee traffic. But since customers visit your machines and not your business, the former isn't an issue. The latter only becomes a problem when you begin to need another pair of hands, by which time you may have outgrown your home anyway. (Caveat: There's usually a provision allowing any number of family members to work for you, regardless of your home office location.)

Many cities' home-business laws are "live and let live," which means compliance with zoning idiosyncrasies is presumed until or unless there's a complaint. This makes good neighborhood relations the key. Talking to those immediately around you and addressing their concerns can go a long way, particularly if you're one of the many vending businesses that doesn't require deliveries from large semis. On the other hand, if you live next door to the Grinch, it's not worth pushing the envelope.

But don't get discouraged before checking the facts. For nine years, Becky P. operated her ever-growing operation out of her home and 700-square-foot RV garage. By the time she moved into a commercial location, she had six employees, in addition to herself and her husband.

"Our home office was on two-thirds of an acre on a main highway," says Becky. "We were lucky to have that type of location. I think it would be very difficult inside a close-knit neighborhood—who wants a semi pulling up at 6:30 in the morning?"

For more on this and a wealth of other home office tips, consult Entrepreneur's business start-up guide No. 1815, *Starting & Running Your Homebased Business*.

Permits and Such

While you're at city hall, ask about permits and licenses. Some municipalities require a general business license while others require registration of each vendor. In the latter case, you may be provided with stickers to affix to the machines. If so, don't cut corners. Failing to affix the stickers can invalidate insurance or open cans of things far worse than worms.

For food vending, you'll need a food handling license either from the U.S. Department of Agriculture or the municipality where your vendors are placed. Generally, you need one or the other but not both, according to NAMA. To be certain, ask each city (or, in rural areas, county) where your machines will be located.

When you've finished with local agencies, you're almost through with officialdom. Only sales taxes remain. Because vending is an automated retail transaction, it's subject to sales taxes, if your state collects them. After you've obtained your name registration certificate, contact your state's department of revenue and ask for sales tax permit application forms.

Covering Yourself: Insurance

Our society's litigiousness is no secret and neither is the cost of guarding against it. Therefore, your final structural concern is insurance.

"If you're going into food, start off with $2 million in liability insurance coverage right away," advises Donald Blotner of DCB Consulting in Eagan, Minnesota. "You can go with less, but what's the point of risking the time and money you have invested in your business by skimping on coverage in an industry known to take big hits in court?"

> **Tip...**
>
> **Smart Tip**
> Check with your state's vending association to find out about sales tax savings strategies. For example, Hendersonville, Tennessee, full-line operator B.J. S. reports his business is paying a tax of 1.5 percent on gross receipts rather than the regular 8.25 percent sales tax. "To be eligible, all we have to do is purchase a $1 sticker for each machine."

▲

Bright Idea

To keep his workers' compensation premiums in check, Hendersonville, Tennessee, full-line operator B.J. S. offers injured employees assistance or time off. "I haven't had any workers' comp claims since I bought the company. If somebody's hurt or doesn't feel well, we have a supervisor help them out. Or if they need it, we give them time off."

This sage advice also applies to other types of vending, according to operators. However, in nonfood vending, slightly less coverage may do. "I carry $1 million in commercial vending machine liability insurance," says Baltimore entrepreneur Janice M. "That's $1 million per incident, per person, per machine."

In some regions, purchasing liability coverage is more than wise: It's required to get your foot in the door. "Here in California, any business of any consequence requires $1 to $2 million in liability insurance before you can do business on their premises," says Becky P. "That's not just for vending operators, but for any outside vendor."

Successful operators also suggest commercial vehicle insurance, which generally goes well beyond personal policies. And regardless of your location, building and contents insurance is a must.

"Within my building insurance, I have a business interruption rider to prevent downtime," comments Becky. "For example, if this place burned to the ground, I would immediately get a $20,000 check to go buy more merchandise and keep the vehicles running. I wouldn't have to go through the investigation and all that stuff before I'd get any money. My insurance company will just instantly keep me up and running."

While operators are quick to value insurance for themselves, mention workers' compensation and the gripe-fest begins. Regardless of vending type, those with employees are subject to this much-maligned coverage.

But industry associations and publications point out that high workers' comp premiums are as much the fault of employers as employees. According to *Automatic Merchandiser* magazine, vending industry premiums soared for years in part because employers failed to teach and enforce simple safety practices. More recently, employers have become hip to the "experience modification" discount (legalese for establishing and following an employee safety plan), which has improved overall safety dramatically and lowered industry premiums. The publication also notes that successful operators involve their employees in safety policy making and evangelizing. After all, reduced comp costs translate into higher profits, which, in turn, means more profit sharing.

Be certain you know all there is to know about insurance. Then use the "Start-Up Checklist" on page 50 to make sure you've covered all your bases in the areas of business structure, naming your business, licensing requirements, zoning regulations, buying insurance, and hiring advisors.

Protecting Your Inspiration: Patent It

As you know from Chapter 1, women's hosiery entrepreneur Janice M. hit on a new vending concept and struck out to fulfill the need she had uncovered. As part of her discovery process, she learned no one else held a U.S. patent on the pantyhose vending concept. Realizing all her work could be in vain if someone swooped down and snapped up her idea, she asked how she could obtain a patent.

"I asked for a package on how to register the trademark," she recalls. "Then I found it was a long hard process. But I realized all I really needed was a disclosure document."

In plain English, the disclosure document allowed Janice to obtain a patent by simply accepting the existing description of a vending machine, as recorded at the patent office, and defining her idea of putting pantyhose and vending together. Within a few short months, she was set—patent and all.

Getting Good Advice

By now you're probably wondering where to turn for help with all these matters. Here's where the cost of hiring an expert pays dividends in the long run.

Successful operators look to professionals for accounting, legal, and insurance advice. For some, this means consulting such gurus directly. For others, it's through the services of industry-specific organizations like NAMA. Still others use general business associations such as their local chamber of commerce or a government-sponsored organization such as the Small Business Administration (SBA).

Of course, you might want to consider a combination of one or more of these avenues. For example, NAMA offers sample client contracts and accounting practices booklets. To customize such items, NAMA members may utilize advisors affiliated with the organization. Or you can hire a local professional to review your situation.

Even more creative is Janice M.'s solution. She surrounds herself with not only advisors, but mentors. The pantyhose vending trailblazer began by tapping into the tax, legal, and accounting assistance offered by the Women Entrepreneurs of Baltimore, one of the organizations she belongs to. Later, she consulted the SBA for financing, the National Association for the Advancement of Colored People for business development assistance, and a brokerage firm about taking her business public. Today she has an accountant, an attorney, an insurance agent, and a Web site designer and counts the editor of *Black Enterprise*

Dollar Stretcher

Before hiring professionals, find out if assistance is available from public or private business organizations and community colleges. In addition to providing free or reduced-fee advice, such organizations can offer referral recommendations and introduce you to invaluable mentoring relationships.

magazine as a significant mentor. "He did a story on me, and the more he tapped into what I did, the more he said, 'This is impressive,' " Janice recalls. "We have remained friends over the years and chat regularly."

Other businesspeople in your community may be able to recommend advisors.

With your structural strategies under control, you are now ready to take your next steps. The issues discussed here should be the only ones you need to address. However, the types of vending operations and laws regulating them are as diverse as the culture we live in. Seeking out specifics that apply to your situation will ensure that you get all your i's dotted and t's crossed.

Start-Up Checklist

Use this handy checklist to help you cover all the regulatory, insurance, and other structural issues.

Yes! I have:

❑ Decided on a business structure: sole proprietorship, partnership, or corporation

❑ Filed the necessary forms to become a partnership or corporation, if I chose either of those structures

❑ Registered my business name

❑ Applied for business licenses in the municipalities where I'll be placing vendors

❑ Investigated zoning regulations

❑ Consulted with a business insurance agent about liability, building, equipment, workers' compensation, and other necessary insurance

❑ Complied with the following special circumstances:

_____

_____

_____

_____

_____

_____

❑ Considered establishing a relationship with an accountant and an attorney

You'll Need
Cash

Although you know going into business isn't going to be free, perhaps you aren't so sure when to begin crunching numbers or what numbers you need to crunch. So before we delve any deeper into the details of starting a vending operation, let's take a look at how you're going to figure out what it's all going to cost. And more important, how you're going to pay for it.

Photo© PhotoDisc Inc.

Start-Up Costs

All the things you absolutely need to open your doors for business are referred to as start-up costs. Not surprisingly, what these costs add up to depends on how big your business is, where it's located, etc.

An attractive reason to go into the vending business in the first place is that one of these expenses, your office, doesn't have to cost any more than you're already paying right now. Why? Because you can operate right out of your home.

Of course, you'll need to invest in vendors and products to put in them. "You can start up for as little as $1,000," says 20-year veteran Wayne D., who points out that bottlers provide machines for free but take a significant cut. "It depends on the magnitude of the business," continues the Burnsville, Minnesota, full-line operator. "That's what makes vending unique."

To give some food vending examples, Wayne throws out some common scenarios. "Let's say I have a friend with a manufacturing business with 300 people. That could be an excellent location for a small start-up, and for that many people, the [vending] equipment would be about $25,000. Or let's say my friend has 20 apartment buildings instead. Then I could probably get by with $15,000 in equipment. It all depends on how well you research the locations and how well you could do there."

But realistically, most operators say launching a viable food vending business requires a bit more. "For a snack and soda business, I'd say $100,000 working capital," advises Northridge, California, full-line operator Becky P., who bucked conventional wisdom by immediately offering sandwiches and other full-line cold food items. "And $250,000 if you're going into full-line. To keep the business running you've got to have a year's worth of money for living expenses in the bank in addition to what you need for your business."

With telecards, it's a similar story. "If you have one two-column machine, you're not going to make enough money to pay for that machine in much under 10 to 12 months," Preston, Washington, telecard operator Pat W. explains. "That means 10 to 12 months before you pay back your savings account. Then you have to save up for 10 to 12 more months to buy your second machine."

In addition, there's product expense. For example, for a telecard machine that dispenses $10 cards and $20 cards, it would require $1,000 to put in 40 cards worth $10 each and 30 cards worth $20 each. "That's for one fill of the machine," Pat stresses. "Say you get a lot of traffic and you sell out. The next time you fill the machine, you need to have [already purchased] more inventory. That's before you've ever collected any money out of the machine, so you don't have a start-up cost of $1,000; it's $2,000 because you have to have enough on hand to refill the machine."

The Bigger Picture

On top of equipment and inventory, you'll also have expenses related to setting up your home office, such as a desk and some file boxes. Then there are other operating costs, such as insurance and sales taxes. We'll discuss more about figuring all of these costs and provide you with some concrete examples in subsequent chapters.

For now, let's introduce you to the two hypothetical start-up vending operations we're going to follow throughout the rest of this book. Giving you these two concrete examples should significantly demystify the start-up process and clarify all those book-keeping and accounting terms we'll run into as we go along. It'll also give you confidence with these matters, which helps as much with winning new customers as it does with romancing the bank.

> **Tip...**
>
> **Smart Tip**
> Shop around for a lender early on, and select one you feel comfortable chatting with. Then schedule a review of your personal finances. This allows you to make necessary adjustments to improve what's referred to as your "net worth" before you lay out your finances for a loan review committee.

▲

1. *Quality Snacks.* Quality Snacks is a homebased vending business with 15 snack vendors. It is operated out of the owner's spare bedroom. The garage has also been pressed into service as a storage location for vendors when they're between accounts as well as a workspace for minor repairs. The garage also houses excess inventory, although almost all inventory fits in the owner's van and is replenished every day, as needed. The total square footage of space used for the business (spare bedroom and garage) is about one-sixth of the total square footage of home and garage combined, or approximately 16 percent. Because the owner of Quality Snacks has a family, a van has been leased and dedicated to the business and a second telephone line goes only to the office space to keep youngsters from answering important calls. Quality Snacks' owner does not draw a salary, instead taking a portion of the net as income. As a start-up, the business is part time, with machine servicings limited to evenings and weekends to accommodate the owner's full-time job.

2. *QuickCard.* Similar to Quality Snacks, QuickCard is a homebased business, but the product is telecards and the machines number ten. It is operated out of a section of the owner's living room, and some closet space for storage is also required. Unlike Quality Snacks, QuickCard's inventory is compact and the machines are smaller. In addition, the owner lives alone in a condominium unit and is retired. Therefore, a previously purchased sedan is sufficient for the part-time business and is also available to the owner for personal use. The portion of the home used for business is about one-fifth of the square footage, or 20 percent.

Allocating Expenses

Take a look at pages 56 and 57 for the "Start-Up Expenses" exhibits of both businesses. Notice some of the line items have been compiled from the expense statements in Chapters 7, 8, 9, and 15. You're welcome to peek at these supporting documents now, or take the numbers on faith and wait 'til we cover the subjects individually, later.

Perhaps one of the first things you'll notice are line items for rent and utilities. This is because a portion of each of these is attributable to the business for tax and accounting purposes. For example, your home office space requires cleaning just as a commercial office space would. Thus, the only way to accurately figure costs is to allocate some funds toward supplies you'll need to buy to keep the dust off your computer, clean dirt from your floor, and remove coffee spills from your carpet.

Bright Idea

If you choose a lender that specializes in business banking, you'll find your banker is an invaluable source of expertise, advice, and professional referrals for every aspect of your operation.

You may be wondering why QuickCard shows telephone expenses despite not having a business telephone line. This is because other types of communication are included as business expenses, such as long-distance calls to suppliers and a cellular phone.

On page 58, you will find a "Start-Up Expenses Worksheet" you may adapt and use to figure your own start-up costs. Of course, you'll find blank supporting worksheets in their appropriate chapters.

What About the Long Haul?

In addition to calculating what you need to start, you'll want to figure out what you can expect to take in from month to month and year to year. This is referred to as your "operating income and expenses." Put more plainly, it's what your operating brings in, what it pays out, and what's left at the end.

Why would you take time to assess this now? Two reasons. First, you'll want to see whether all the effort you're about to put into the business is worth the return. Some entrepreneurs feel successful when they've broken even; others have certain profit goals in mind. Because everyone's different, only you can determine if the return on your investment is appropriate for the price. The second reason is your bank or leasing or financing company. These institutions live and die by columns of numbers. They know from time-honored experience the only way to judge whether a business is worth investing in (read: lending money to) is by getting the numbers down on paper. If you create both a start-up expenses statement and an operating income and expense statement before you set foot in your lender's office, you will be showing them you speak their language and are thus more deserving of their trust.

Check out pages 61 and 63 for projected operating budgets for Quality Snacks and QuickCard. Again, the information is drawn from details we'll discuss in Chapters 7, 8, 9, and 15. Essentially, the numbers you see here are the result of taking the sample monthly income and expense statements we compiled on pages 194 and 196 in Chapter 15 and multiplying them by 12 (the number of months in a year). By calculating an expected operating budget for an entire year, you can figure out how much (if any) you'll need to have in the bank, from a lender, or through another income source to cover your regular living expenses.

Lease, Borrow, or Buy?

Once you have added all your expenses, the next step is deciding whether or not you can afford the bottom line. If the numbers look too large for what you've saved or think you can borrow, consider starting smaller or saving a bit longer before you begin.

According to industry statistics, your average rate of return (the percentage you have left over of the income you make) will likely be less than 4 percent. Some of the successful operators we interviewed say their average is between .5 percent and 2 percent.

Quality Snacks Start-Up Expenses

Below is the start-up expenses statement for our hypothetical snack food oper-ator, Quality Snacks. For a description of Quality Snacks, see "The Bigger Picture" section on page 53.

Expense	Cost
Advertising/marketing	$100.00
CPA/accounting	150.00
Insurance	500.00
Inventory (from Chapter 9)	4,588.00
Licenses and fees	300.00
Office equipment and supplies (from Chapter 7)	3,041.00
Rent	100.00
Subscriptions/dues	200.00
Telephone	90.00
Utilities	30.00
Vehicle lease	500.00
Vending equipment (from Chapter 8)	73,960.00
Subtotal	$83,559.00
Other miscellaneous expenses (add roughly 10 percent of the subtotal)	8,356.00
Total Start-Up Costs	**$91,915.00**
Owner's contribution	$74,415.00
Financing required (vendors)	$17,500.00

QuickCard Start-Up Expenses

Below is the start-up expenses statement for our hypothetical telecard operator, QuickCard. For a description of QuickCard, see "The Bigger Picture" section on page 53.

Expense	Cost
Advertising/marketing	$50.00
CPA/accounting	0
Insurance	250.00
Inventory (from Chapter 9)	8,835.00
Licenses and fees	50.00
Office equipment and supplies (from Chapter 7)	653.00
Rent	75.00
Subscriptions/dues	200.00
Telephone	25.00
Utilities	25.00
Vehicle lease	0
Vending equipment (from Chapter 8)	16,500.00
Subtotal	$26,663.00
Other miscellaneous expenses (add roughly 10 percent of the subtotal)	2,666.00
Total Start-Up Costs	**$29,329.00**
Owner's contribution	$24,229.00
Financing required (vendors)	$5,100.00

Start-Up Expenses Worksheet

Here's a handy guide for figuring the start-up costs for your business. For a nifty note sheet, photocopy this page before you begin. To make your calculating even easier, come back to this form after you've completed the supporting worksheets in the related chapters and reviewed the helpful tips in the book sections covering line items such as marketing, insurance, and the like.

Expense	Cost
Advertising/marketing	
CPA/accounting	
Insurance	
Inventory (from Chapter 9)	
Licenses and fees	
Office equipment and supplies (from Chapter 7)	
Rent	
Subscriptions/dues	
Telephone	
Utilities	
Vehicle lease	
Vending equipment (from Chapter 8)	
Subtotal	
Other miscellaneous expenses (add roughly 10 percent of the subtotal)	
Total Start-Up Costs	
Owner's contribution	
Financing required (vendors)	

Therefore, be careful before you assume you'll simply get a loan.

"If it's going to cost you 10 percent to borrow money and your average return is 3 to 4 percent, it doesn't take a brain surgeon…," says Hendersonville, Tennessee, full-line operator B.J. S. "It's better to have start-up capital to buy the machines upfront. Your inheritance, your 401(k), or whatever it is. If you borrow money and put machines in locations that don't work, then you fail. I've seen so many people selling machines, getting out of vending, and swearing they'll never do it again."

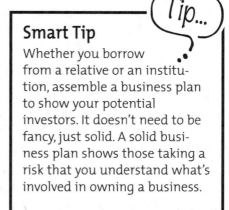

Smart Tip

Whether you borrow from a relative or an institution, assemble a business plan to show your potential investors. It doesn't need to be fancy, just solid. A solid business plan shows those taking a risk that you understand what's involved in owning a business.

That said, most operators admit they did borrow funds. "I borrowed from family, had some savings, and have some loans," Becky P. says. "But I pay off the loans in half the time."

Lines of credit are also an option. With a line of credit, you only owe money when you've borrowed, much like a credit card. A line of credit from a bank generally carries much lower interest rates and fees than loans. "I have a $65,000 line of credit," says Becky. "If I want to dump $5,000 [of debt] one month, I can. Or if I only want to pay the interest one month, I can."

Vending is risky for banks because their collateral (your vendors) can be removed and stashed out of sight to keep them from being repossessed. "You have to have an excellent credit rating," stresses Becky, who had borrowed and repaid several bank loans before going into vending. "With my business background, I never had a problem going into my bank and selling myself. In fact, when banks started giving lines of credit, the manager came over [to my office] and said, 'I want you to have this because you run your business properly.'"

Your Distributor Can Help

If you're an unknown quantity at the bank, don't conclude you're out of luck. Instead, talk to your equipment distributor.

"Typically, a piece of equipment will be financed for two years," notes Vince Gumma of American Vending Sales in Chicago. "The average payment is $165 a month." If you're lacking capital to make a down payment but your business plan looks viable, you may be granted financing with a large final payment at the end of the financing period. In such cases, the last payment is often 10 to 20 percent of the total amount you're borrowing.

Of course, your best bet for winning the approval of your distributor's financing company is still to have collateral of your own to offer, such as equity in your home.

Underfunding Undertow

Regardless of your source of cash, the most important thing when it comes to financing a business is having enough. Many former business owners would be a successful entrepreneur today if they hadn't underestimated and underfinanced.

Those who do make it despite being underfunded generally would avoid making the same mistake twice. "Before [I went out and raised funds] I was using my own money," recounts Baltimore pantyhose operator Janice M., who is blazing her own trail by designing a unique pantyhose vendor and vending machine business. In addition to income from her administrative assistant position, the single mother of three was also maxing out her credit cards. "I was going through getting my gas and my electricity shut off. But I just tried to stay focused to get done what I wanted to do."

Soon after her finances hit bottom, Janice began looking for private investors. "Most of them were working people," says Janice, some of whom generously gave as little as $25. "One man saw me making something happen and gave me $5,000." In all, the vending innovator raised $14,000, which helped carry her through her business' second and third years. "Later I also went to the Women Entrepreneurs of Baltimore [a nonprofit business development group she belonged to] and they gave me $1,000." At the time of this writing, Janice was working with her bank on more financing to help her expand her 12-machine line.

Dollar Stretcher

Taking advantage of those incessant credit card solicitations you receive in the mail can provide you with some financing flexibility, but don't go hog wild. Banks and other financing sources often shy away from people with the potential to run up excessive credit card debt.

Quality Snacks Projected Operating Budget

Below is the projected operating budget for the first year of operation of our snack food operator, Quality Snacks. For a description of Quality Snacks, see "The Bigger Picture" on page 53.

Income	
Machine sales	$115,200.00
Other income	0
Total Annual Income	**$115,200.00**
Expenses	
Advertising/marketing	210.00
Commissions	11,520.00
CPA/accounting	240.00
Depreciation	
Office equipment/furnishings	576.00
Vehicles	0
Vendors	4,608.00
Insurance	1,200.00
Licenses and fees	600.00
Office expenses	
Equipment/furnishings	120.00
Office supplies	243.60
Rent	1,200.00
Repairs/maintenance	240.00
Telephone	960.00
Utilities	360.00

Quality Snacks Projected Operating Budget, continued

Payroll	$0
Product expenses	
Cost of goods sold	57,600.00
Product loss	2,400.00
Professional services (including contract)	300.00
Sales/use taxes	9,216.00
Subscriptions/dues	270.00
Travel, meals, entertainment	0
Vehicle expenses	
Lease payments	6,000.00
Maintenance and repair	3,000.00
Vending equipment expenses	
Machine loans (5 machines)	9,900.00
Parts and repairs	230.40
Storage	0
Delivery/moving/freight	600.00
Other miscellaneous expenses	309.00
Total Annual Expenses	**$111,903.00**
Net annual profit (loss) before taxes	3,297.00
Income tax (estimated)	372.68
Net Annual Profit (Loss) After Taxes	**$2,924.32**

QuickCard Projected Operating Budget

Below is the projected operating budget for the first year of operation of our snack food operator, QuickCard. For a description of QuickCard, see "The Bigger Picture" on page 53.

Income	
Machine sales	$112,500.00
Other income	1,200.00
Total Annual Income	**$113,700.00**
Expenses	
Advertising/marketing	120.00
Commissions	22,740.00
CPA/accounting	0
Depreciation	
Office equipment/furnishings	113.76
Vehicles	568.56
Vendors	2,274.00
Insurance	540.00
Licenses and fees	84.00
Office expenses	
Office supplies	123.60
Rent	900.00
Repairs/maintenance	60.00
Telephone	540.00
Utilities	180.00
Payroll	0

Quickcard Projected Operating Budget, continued

Product expenses	
Cost of goods sold	$ 70,494.00
Product loss	120.00
Professional services (including contract)	360.00
Sales/use taxes	7,959.00
Subscriptions/dues	216.00
Travel, meals, entertainment	0
Vehicle expenses	
Lease payments	0
Maintenance and repair	600.00
Vending equipment expenses	
Machine loans (three 4-column)	2,952.00
Parts and repairs	60.00
Storage	0
Delivery/moving/freight	600.00
Other miscellaneous expenses	0
Total Annual Expenses	**$111,604.92**
Net annual profit (loss) before taxes	2,095.08
Income tax (estimated)	236.82
Net Annual Profit (Loss) After Taxes	**$1,858.26**

Projected Operating Budget Worksheet

Here's a handy guide for figuring your projected operating budget for your first year in business. The easiest way to crunch the numbers is to use the data entered on the one-month "Income and Expense Statement Worksheet" in Chapter 15 and multiply each line item by 12.

Income	
Machine sales	
Other income	
Total Annual Income	
Expenses	
Advertising/marketing	
Bank service charges	
Commissions	
CPA/accounting	
Depreciation	
Office equipment/furnishings	
Vehicles	
Vending machines	
Insurance	
Licenses and fees	
Office expenses	
Equipment/furnishings	
Office supplies	
Rent	
Repairs/maintenance	
Telephone	
Utilities	
Payroll	
Salaries/wages	
Benefits	

Projected Operating Budget Worksheet, continued

Payroll taxes	
Workers' comp	
Product expenses	
Cost of goods sold	
Product loss	
Professional services(including contract)	
Sales/use taxes	
Subscriptions/dues	
Travel, meals, entertainment	
Vehicle expenses	
Vehicle purchases	
Lease payments	
Loan payments—principle	
Loan payments—interest	
Maintenance and repair	
Vending equipment expenses	
Machine purchases	
Lease payments	
Loan payments—principle	
Loan payments—interest	
Parts and repairs	
Storage	
Delivery/moving/freight	
Other miscellaneous expenses	
Total Annual Expenses	
Net annual profit (loss) before taxes	
Income tax (estimated)	
Net Annual Profit (Loss) After Taxes	

7

Office, Sweet
Office

It's no secret—vending success requires being out and about. The more vendors you own, the more money you make. It's as simple as that.

Therefore, getting to (and working in) the office is downtime. Swanky digs are irrelevant because your customers visit your machines and not you. And even if you grow to be a multimillion-dollar operation, you'll rarely, if ever, entertain clients on-site. Thus, vending always has been, and probably always will be, a perfect business to start in your home.

The Home Front

Not only do most vending businesses begin as homebased, but successful entrepreneurs stress the cost advantages of an in-home location. "What people don't realize [about vending] is that all you get to keep is a half-cent of every dollar you make," says Northridge, California, full-line operator Becky P. "If you're extremely successful, you might make one to two cents. Working out of the house was a godsend for us. When you're struggling, trying to cover overhead rent [in addition to your mortgage or apartment payments] is very difficult. Having a homebased business helps tremendously by keeping overhead down."

Of course, at some point, you may outgrow your in-home setup. Or if you're getting into vending by purchasing an existing outfit, maybe a home office is already out of the question. But no matter where your office is located, here are some tips on getting it appointed.

Homebased Basics

Because so few vending activities are desk-centric, don't worry about devoting an enormous area of your home to an office space. A corner of your kitchen is just as viable as a finished room over your garage.

What's important is a location that makes administrative minutes count. Sharing the living room with your children's Nintendo game or *101 Dalmatians* video won't encourage productivity or produce sounds you want clients to hear in the background. If you have an active family, look for a quiet zone, like a corner of your bedroom, which allows you to step inside and shut the door.

"When I go in my office, my kids know I'm in there to work," says Baltimore operator Janice M., a single mother of three. "When I go in and close the door, I really feel like I've stepped into the office. And when I leave it, I can go into another part of my house and really feel like I'm at home. I think that's really essential. You have to find a place to go that you consider your office space."

Stashing Your Stuff

But what about storage? After all, vending is an inventory-intensive business. What do you do with your products before you load them into your vehicle?

In the past, a homebased vending business required a garage or other significant warehousing space. However, vending today is increasingly a "just in time" industry.

"We have a cash and carry service where operators come in and shop just as in a grocery store," asserts John Ochi of Vernon Hills, Illinois-based Five Star Distributors. "Then you don't require a warehouse—you use our warehouse. A number of operators who use our cash and carry service are not only in vending full time, they even have one or two employees."

For compact products, such as telecards or pantyhose, a closet (or even part of one) is enough for inventory. Then your only issue is vendors. "When I didn't have room to store a shipment of machines, I rented a friend's bedroom for a month," confides Preston, Washington, telecard operator Pat W. "She was glad to get the $50, which was half the cost of using a mini-storage [facility], and my machines weren't out in the rain."

With life expectancies rising and more seniors staying in their homes, ferreting out storage space doesn't necessarily mean turning to a friend. Seniors on fixed incomes are often happy to rent space in their garages, basements, or spare bedrooms. Visit a luncheon at your senior center or post a notice through your place of worship to find empty-nesters with room to share.

Taxing Advantages

Home offices also present operators with important tax advantages. Just as the IRS permits businesses to write off the cost of an office located in a commercial property, it also allows deductions for maintaining one at home. The amount you may deduct is based on what portion of your home you use as an income-generating office. Let's say you turn a 12 foot by 12 foot spare bedroom into an office. If the total finished area of your home is 960 square feet, then your business portion is 15 percent. Thus, you may deduct 15 percent of your rent, utilities, repairs, maintenance (including cleaning!), and various other incidentals.

What's the catch? The portion you deduct must be *exclusively* used for business. The same goes for a separate structure, such as a garage, and storage space, such as closets.

Does this mean you can't deduct a nook in the kitchen or the closet full of inventory in the hall? Not exactly. You may *not* include any part of your kitchen (or the closet) used for nonbusiness activities (even if your dining table doubles as your coin counting area).

Tip...

Smart Tip

If your office is a portion of a room, it's still easy to document business-use square footage for the IRS. Place several yardsticks or tape measures on the floor to delineate the area. Be conservative. Then, take close-up photographs of the space with the yardsticks in view, as well as some 360-degree shots of the entire room.

However, if the nook is *only* used for your business, you may use its square footage to figure the portion of your home used *exclusively* as an office.

For more on this and a wealth of other home office tips, consult Entrepreneur's business start-up guide No. 1815, *Starting & Running Your Homebased Business.*

Decking It Out

Furnish your office with the basics—a desk and a chair. You're not impressing clients, and you won't spend hours on your fanny, so whatever's functional will do. A desk need be no fancier than an old door supported by cinder blocks or a 6-foot folding banquet table found at most office superstores. For a chair, commandeer the one you save for unexpected Thanksgiving guests. Remember, margins in vending are as narrow as any in retail, so it pays to start out humble.

Paperwork storage is next. Resurrecting a rusty file cabinet stashed in your basement or the corner of a pawn shop is one option. Cardboard file boxes from the local office superstore is another. You won't be drowning in paperwork, but you will need a home for client contracts, route cards, utility bills, inventory invoices, and the like.

Counting Coin

Depending on the size of your operation and the type of products you vend, you may need a coin or currency counter. "As they grow, lots of vendors sell their old coin/currency counter sets," says Becky P. "A good used set starts around $1,000."

For the telecard operator, it's strictly manual. "I have all paper money—no coins," Pat W. says. "And I have a whole bunch of rubber bands."

If you'd still like to mechanize your counting activities, but the budget's tight, you'll find new low-end, coin-only models cost about $35.

After you count your cash, you must total it up. Grabbing your kid's pocket calculator is a cost-free option. But the slip of a digit sets you back to square one. Stick with a basic adding machine, with paper tape, for about $25.

No matter how you add it all up, ask your bank in advance how it wants your coins and currency. "Banks are very particular," says Pat W. "They like to have money bundled in a certain way. You may be bringing in several thousand dollars at a time and [your bank's employees] have to count it."

Beware!

For most of us, it's tempting to blow off establishing a filing system. Even a few folders grouped broadly by category, such as "income," "credit card bills," "equipment invoices," and "inventory expenses," save you from hours of productivity-robbing headaches at tax time.

I'm on the Phone

Unless you live alone, at least one phone line dedicated to your business is simply a fact of life. While subscribing to voice mail can eliminate busy signals, you must monitor your messages. Constantly wrestling your teenagers or your spouse to check your messages, make calls, or send faxes is unproductive, to say the least.

Dollar Stretcher

Because most homebased vending operations aren't fax-intensive, your business line can double as your fax line in the beginning. Give voice communications priority by relegating most faxing to evenings and weekends.

Get a two-line phone for your office and put both your home and business phone on it. Then, you can use your home phone for outgoing calls, and save your business line for incoming. In nonoffice areas, stick to a one-line unit to avoid apologizing for your 6-year-old's answering etiquette.

For all the times you're out of the office or, invariably, you're stepping into the bathroom, get automated. "You need an answering machine or voice mail," says Burnsville, Minnesota, full-line operator Wayne D. "When people call about an out-of-service machine, they want it fixed now."

A second phone line will cost about $30 a month plus an installation fee of about $40. Check with your local provider to be sure. A two-line phone with minimal features, such as a speakerphone, runs less than $50. If you go with an answering machine, add a one-time cost of $20. Voice mail averages $6 to $20 monthly. If you choose the answering machine route, heed this advice: Know the limits of your system. Answering machines that record messages on tape are safer than those that save them digitally. No matter what the manual indicates, power surges and power failures are notorious memory-wipers.

Whatever you decide, remember that vending is intensely competitive. Exceptional customer service separates the successful from the also-rans. Skimping on phone lines (or answering devices) to save pennies costs dollars in the end.

Wireless Wonders

Why wireless? "I have to be the sales team and the marketing team and everything," explains Janice M. "Even though I have an office, I'm never really in one spot. I want people to be able to [reach] me."

Cellular phones can be an operator's best friend, minimizing the impact of mechanical malfunctions. "Today's machines are so computerized that the manufacturer's technicians ask you to punch in things to get a readout of what is wrong—motor error, solenoid error, etc.," says Becky P. "But you have to be standing at that machine with the capability to punch stuff in."

Although cellular phones are hip, consider a pager if you are starting out as a part-time operator while you work at another job. You will know when customers call without irritating your boss. Whether you select a cell or go with a pager, give your customers the option of accessing you immediately by integrating your wireless number into your voice-mail greeting. To get wired, look for a cellular provider who throws in the phone, voice mail, and other goodies for free when you sign up for service. Also, as the competition intensifies, more and more local telephone companies are offering deals that combine traditional phone and wireless services at a price that is tough to beat. For wireless alone, figure on about $30 to $50 a month.

The Great Computer Debate

For most pieces of office equipment, recommendations are nearly universal. But for computers, you'll hear strong arguments from both sides of the aisle.

According to 20-year operating veteran Wayne D., computerizing was the most important factor in his business' success. "At the time, we didn't really understand the impact it had or the ability it gave to manage your business so much better."

Janice M. agrees. "Before I started using a computer, I found myself constantly reordering things that weren't selling." In addition to straightening out her inventory, computerization also allows the Baltimore operator to produce her own stationery, market research surveys, contracts, customer feedback forms, and even colorful sales presentations.

Another argument for computers is Internet access. For instance, if your prospects are contacts at large companies, it's likely they will be accustomed to doing business via e-mail. When choosing between you and another operator, ease of communication may tip the scales. For more information on the marketing and customer service implications of computers and the Internet, see Chapters 12 and 14.

On the other hand, Pat W. believes in pen and paper. "I've never computerized," says the retiree who vends telecards. "I do all my accounting by hand and keep it in a record book."

Industry consultant and former operator Don Blotner of DCB Consulting in Eagan, Minnesota, supports Pat W.'s view. "What's mission-critical for a new operator is getting and servicing new accounts. To be successful, you must get larger—fast. Everything else is

Beware!

If the rebates on your PC look too good to be true, they probably are. Internet access providers (companies you pay to board the information superhighway) want your account so badly they'll offer hundreds of dollars off your computer purchase. Read the fine print. Most of these contracts require a multiyear minimum at a total cost that far exceeds the rebate amount.

secondary. Whether you track your own finances on paper or use some type of software depends on how comfortable you are with technology."

If you decide to go with a computer, forget the mean multimedia machine. Instead, approach the question from a usage angle. "You basically need a software program that you can get started with and continue to build on as you continue to grow your business," advises Wayne D.

Dollar Stretcher

Never limit yourself to buying only at office superstores. Discount department stores offer budget office furnishings, and sometimes you will pay less than you would have at your local superstore.

Another way to computerize without breaking the bank is with a refurbished machine. Recycled systems are increasingly popular as hardware technology outpaces the functions many computer users need. To run a spreadsheet or, for novices, a small-business accounting program, stay with a simple system and expect to pay around $1,000.

For a vending-specific resource on PCs, the "Computer System Checklist," turn to pages 74 and 75.

Fax/Copier Conundrum

The only other pieces of equipment to consider are a fax machine for communicating with customers and suppliers, and a copier. According to operators, both are handy but not imperative. But as soon as you become a regular at your local copy/fax shop, it's time to re-evaluate. Remember, attending to administrative details detracts from filling machines and, therefore, profits.

Plain-paper fax machines also handle basic copier chores and list for under $150. If you are computerizing, you can save a bundle by investing in an all-in-one printer/fax/copier/scanner. In addition to being easy on the budget, these multifunction machines are also space-savers.

Going Commercial

Although it's likely your homebased office will fit perfectly for years and years, every rule has its exceptions. If you're one of them, you'll have to go commercial.

A multiplex office/warehouse facility is a good choice. "We're very pleased here," says Becky P. "We have about 2,100 square feet, office and warehouse combined. We lease the space, and it costs us about $1,400 a month."

If you purchase an operation that is already in a building, there is still an overhead-abatement option, according to Hendersonville, Tennessee, full-line operator

Computer System Checklist

Use this handy checklist when you go computer shopping.

Essential Hardware

- ❏ Pentium processor (any type and speed)
- ❏ 128MB RAM
- ❏ 8MB graphics (aka "video card")
- ❏ 4GB hard drive (any speed)
- ❏ 3.5" floppy drive
- ❏ 15" monitor
- ❏ CD-RW* drive (any speed)
- ❏ Keyboard
- ❏ Mouse (with mouse pad)
- ❏ 56K fax/modem (to get on the Internet)

Essential Accessories

- ❏ Surge protector
- ❏ Printer
- ❏ All-in-one multifunction machine (printer, fax, copier, and scanner)

Optional Hardware *(in order of importance)*

- ❏ UPS (uninterruptible power supply—better than a surge protector)
- ❏ Sound card (PCs have minimal sound built-in, but without a sound card, output is limited)
- ❏ Speakers (for sound card)

Essential Software

- ❏ Windows (current version)
- ❏ QuickBooks (or similar novice-friendly accounting software)
- ❏ Antivirus (any)
- ❏ Internet browser

Recommended Software

- ❏ Word processor
- ❏ Spreadsheet program
- ❏ Desktop publisher

CD-RW means "CD rewritable." This is a CD drive that allows you to make and reuse CDs. CD-RW goes beyond CD-ROM, which only reads pre-made disks. It also surpasses CD-R (for "writable"), which permits making a CD but, unlike a floppy, not erasing and starting over. With floppies nearly obsolete due to storage limitations, a CD-RW is a wise investment.

Computer System Checklist, continued

Optional Software

❏ Web page designer

Special considerations for my business or questions I want to ask my computer consultant or salesperson:

_____

_____

_____

_____

_____

_____

_____

_____

_____

_____

_____

B.J. S. "I own the building, personally, and the business rents it from me," explains the operator. "That way, you can set the rent and hopefully build up some of your personal wealth."

No matter where you set up your office, remember the old saying about all work and no play. Eating donuts on Thursdays and playing your favorite CDs are great perks whether you're in-home or out.

Office Equipment Expenses

To help you budget, here are furnishing, equipment, and supply costs for the two fictional vending operations we introduced in Chapter 6, Quality Snacks and QuickCard.

	Quality Snacks	QuickCard
Desk	$60	N/A*
Folding table	N/A	$40
File boxes	N/A	$6
File cabinet	$30	N/A
Phone (two-line with voice mail)	$50	N/A
Answering machine	N/A	$20
Cellular telephone	inc. with service	N/A
Pager	N/A	$40
Fax	N/A	$150
Adding machine with tape	$25	$25
Coin/currency counter, Professional-grade ledger	$1,000	N/A
Ledger book	N/A	$30
Rolodex	$5	$5
Stapler	$7	$7
CD-RW disks (10)	$30	N/A
All-in-one printer/fax/copier/scanner	$299	N/A
Computer system	$1,000	N/A
UPS (uninterruptible power supply)	$90	N/A
Business/marketing software	$250	N/A
Coin wrappers	$10	N/A
Envelopes, plain #10 (box)	$10	$5
Paper, computer/fax/copier (box)	$20	N/A
Stationery, blank (to create letterhead, etc.)	$35	N/A
Stationery, designed and printed at printer	N/A	$250
Miscellaneous office supplies	$100	$75
Total Expenditures	**$3,041**	**$653**

N/A = Not applicable. In other words, this hypothetical operation doesn't own this item.

Office Equipment Worksheet

Here's a handy shopping guide for equipping your office. Although it's designed with the homebased operator in mind, you'll need the same gear if you're in commercial quarters.

For a nifty note sheet, photocopy this page before you begin. Then, when you're finished shopping, total up the costs to give yourself a head start on the "Start-Up Expenses Worksheet" in Chapter 6 on page 58.

Desk	
Folding table	
File boxes	
File cabinet	
Phone (two-line with voice mail)	
Answering machine	
Cellular telephone	
Pager	
Adding machine with tape	
Coin/currency counter. professional-grade	
Coin counter, budget	
Coin sorter tray, manual	
Ledger book (if no computer)	
Rolodex	
Stapler	
Computer system (see "Computer system checklist" on page 73)	
CD-RW disks	
All-in-one printer/fax/copier/scanner	
UPS (uninterruptible power supply)	

Office Equipment Worksheet, continued

Business/marketing software:	
Antivirus	
Small-business accounting	
Office suite (word processor, spreadsheet, desktop publisher)	
Internet browser	
Coin wrappers	
Envelopes, plain #10	
Paper, computer/fax/copier (if computerizing)	
Stationery, blank (to create letterhead, etc.)	
Paper	
Envelopes	
Business cards	
Stationery, designed and printed at printer	
Miscellaneous office supplies (adding machine tape, file folders, etc.)	
Total Expenditures	

Your Vendors
and Your Wheels

W hew" you may be thinking. "We're finally getting to what I wanted to know about in the first place." Or maybe you had noticed this chapter in the Table Of Contents and decided to cut to the chase. Either way, the time to talk vending machine turkey has definitely arrived.

Photo© Automatic Products International Ltd.

As we have said before, vending is a unique form of retailing. Products are sold directly to customers, but there's no sales associate or waitress presenting offerings with a smile. Nor is there a swanky showroom or cool color catalog to make a good first impression. Instead, it's by an inanimate machine that you live and die.

While you can economize by furnishing your home office with a brick-and-board desk, you must think of your vendors as your suit-and-tie sales force. This chapter will tell you what you need to know to help you assemble a winning team of machines. It'll also give you some direction on what kind of transportation you'll need to keep your vending business moving forward.

Automat Axioms

Unless you've lived a fairly sheltered life, you already know vending machines aren't all alike. Some offer a wide variety of products, while others carry only a few. Some sport glass fronts, allowing you to see the Oreos before you buy them, while others only show logos or even simply display words like "coffee, black."

Whether or not you can see what's inside, the "guts" of all machines work similarly. Products are all neatly compartmentalized with a button or a number that corresponds to the product's location. Once that location, or "column," is empty, nothing else will be dispensed from that compartment.

For example, inside a machine that carries cola, root beer and lemonade, there's not a central area from which the unit grabs a root beer when the "root beer" button is pushed. Only the column(s) stocked with root beer dispense(s) that item. In addition, columns can have different capacities, which allows you to place the most popular items in the columns with greatest capacity.

Another important nuance is overall size. Two units standing next to each other may appear to hold the same amount of merchandise. However, one may actually contain half as much as another. While the smaller unit will be less expensive, it's also incapable of growing with your business. In other words, you can purchase a 500-unit snack machine and fill it half full, but you can't expand a 250-unit machine to serve the needs of a more demanding account.

New *vs.* Used

In addition to selecting vendor type and capacity, you'll have to decide on new or used equipment. The answer to "What's the best?" isn't cast in stone, but operators and experts offer some good advice on which direction to go.

For sizable locations, Northridge, California, full-line operator Becky P. recommends something hot off the assembly line. "If you're going in with a full-bank with four or more machines and a location with 100 employees or more, I'd go new."

Why? Like all mechanical devices, new machines run more reliably than old. "Used machines require more service and have more downtime," says Vince Gumma of Chicago's American Vending Sales, distributor of both new and used vendors. "If the machine is down, then you're not making money."

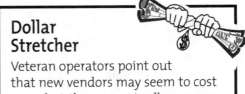

Dollar Stretcher

Veteran operators point out that new vendors may seem to cost more but they can actually save you money. "Over the course of time, having new machines is still cheaper than having to go out and repair them," says Burnsville, Minnesota, full-line operator Wayne D.

For this reason, some operators swear by new equipment regardless of location. "I started with used machines," Burnsville, Minnesota, full-line operator Wayne D. notes. "But based on the differential today, you're only looking at 30 to 40 percent savings. We have 20 times as many machines now as 15 years ago, but we have fewer trouble calls now than then because the equipment is newer."

Attracting and retaining accounts are two more arguments for new. "We buy new equipment because you know what you're getting," says Hendersonville, Tennessee, full-line operator B.J. S. "The [client] is happy to get new equipment, too."

From his vantage point as a product distributor, John Ochi of Vernon Hills, Illinois-based Five Star Distributors observes, "Most people who enter the food businesses buy used. But if you're launching a business where you have an 'in' at a certain facility, such as a software company, you may need what new technology has to offer to satisfy your client and your customers."

Expect to shell out between $1,000 and $7,000 for new food-related machines. For purposes of calculating start-up costs, the average is about $3,500. For telecard machines, use $1,400 as a ballpark figure for a two-column machine and $1,700 for a four-column machine.

Opting for Pre-Owned

As many advantages as there are to new equipment, operators and experts say there are still plenty of reasons to invest in old.

"For a 50-person location, there are properly refurbished machines that are beautiful," comments food vendor Becky P. "But just like when you buy a used car and take it to a mechanic, I'd have someone come look at used machines first. I'd rather spend $50 or $75 to get a technician's opinion than spend $10,000 on vendors that don't work."

If a machine is new enough, it won't even need to be refurbished. In this case, you can get deals by purchasing them from other operators. "Lots of times, you can get good deals on machines from people getting out of the business," Becky explains. "You can find fliers for them in your cash and carries, such as Costco, Sam's Club, or even a vending products distributor."

In fact, Preston, Washington, telecard operator Pat W. built her business on pre-owned machines. "For a long time, I bought used machines from people who had them in their garages."

> **Beware!**
> If you're purchasing used equipment, look for a small plaque with a serial number and date of manufacture. Without these items, it's impossible to tell just how old a machine is and, therefore, the difficulty of finding parts, likelihood for downtime, etc., warns Northridge, California, full-line veteran Becky P. "If the plaque's not there, buyer beware."

In food vending, one way to use pre-owned equipment effectively is in situations Gumma refers to as "overequipped." "For example, maybe you're putting a bank of machines in the break room, but the vice president wants a coffee machine outside his office. In this case, I'd recommend putting a used piece near the VP."

Another key is location profitability. "If the difference in making a location profitable is used instead of new, I'd say you shouldn't be in that location in the first place," asserts Gumma. "If you're that close to the margin, service costs and overhead can quickly make you unprofitable."

A final question to consider is: How old is old? "I don't recommend buying a machine made before about 1992," stresses Becky P. "They began computerizing about that time. Your customers are too sophisticated today—they expect a dollar changer and other modern devices."

Although he sells free-standing bill and coin changing devices, equipment distributor Gumma concurs with Becky's advice. "According to studies, the average American carries 42 cents in his or her pocket," Gumma says. "Today, the average cost of a candy bar or soda is more than 50 cents. If you are dead set on not using a bill acceptor, I would challenge you to walk up to ten people and ask how much money they have in their pocket. Remember, the easier you make it for the consumer, the more sales you'll get."

Should pre-owned be right for you, insist on paying no more than 60 percent of what a similar new model costs.

You Get What You Pay For

Despite the importance of evaluating age, don't let it be the deciding factor. "Just like anything else, you get what you pay for," says Pat W. "With a vending machine, quality always wins out. They're expensive to repair, and if you have trouble with them, it comes right out of your overhead. You need to keep your overhead down. Choosing a dependable and secure machine is a make-or-break decision for your business."

Signs of quality include above-average warranties, 24-hour toll-free technical support, and replacement parts shipped next-day air. Average warranties vary with the type of machine, so ask for spec sheets on every brand you can find and then compare. Pay particular attention to warranties on compressors, which are expensive, and bill acceptors, which are fickle. "Bill acceptors are extremely finicky," Becky P. cautions. "The way they differentiate between denominations is they read the metal in the ink."

To Change or Not to Change

The vagaries of bill acceptors bring up an important point. For food operators planning to serve locations with more than 100 employees or for any size location that includes refrigerated food, relying on a dollar bill acceptor isn't enough.

▲

"If you spend any time in a break room, at some point you'll see somebody with a dollar bill who keeps feeding it into the machine and it doesn't want to take it," states Becky P. "And after the third try they walk out to the door to the catering truck—what does that tell you?

"You don't ever want to lose a sale," she continues. "We do have dollar bill acceptors on everything, but if you have a nasty bill, the ones in the machines aren't as sophisticated as the ones in the [free-standing] changers." Therefore, Becky outfits her lunch room machines with bill acceptors as well as bill and coin changer units that are free-standing.

For food vending machines, a bill acceptor adds approximately $750 to the cost. Free-standing changers average $2,000.

Getting the Goods

If you are not buying directly from another operator, the most common place to acquire new or used vending equipment is a distributor. Distributors can be thought of as a vending department store—they offer machines built by a variety of different manufacturers and for a wide array of specialties.

Like anything you buy, this added layer between you and the producer ultimately increases costs. However, there's also a significant benefit. Because they carry competing manufacturer's wares, distributors can assist you with deciding what's right for your needs. "You should expect your distributor to offer advice and assistance gained from dealing with successful operators," notes Gumma. They should also provide comprehensive training on how to use equipment, perform preventative maintenance, and do routine repairs.

Bright Idea

Seek opinions from well-established operators on the best manufacturers and distributors in your vending specialty. Ask the National Automatic Merchandising Association or a similar trade organization to pair you up with operators outside your competition area, or post a request in an online chat room such as the one maintained by the Vending Connection at www.vending connection.com.

Speaking of repairs, vendors are like cars—the question isn't *if* they'll malfunction, it's *when*. Although you will often troubleshoot by phoning the manufacturer directly, sometimes you'll need hands-on help. "Manufacturers may have one field person for several states," notes distributor Gumma. "A good distributor will have a large inventory of parts and several field technicians devoted to your area."

In addition, you should expect your distributor to assist you with obtaining financing. "They should interview you, collect your financial information, do the legwork required to assemble credit documents, and meet with the finance companies to obtain the best rates," Gumma says. "If an operator's credit is good, they should even be willing to go 'on recourse,' which means they agree to share in the risk of lending the money," he continues. "For example, the financing company may say to the distributor, 'We want you to take 50 percent of this application on recourse.' Although the operator may still have to offer collateral, such as the equity in their home, the distributor agrees to stand behind them."

For an example of the financial information a distributor will expect, check out the American Vending Sales Inc. "Application for Credit" on page 95.

To locate distributors offering equipment in your specialty area, consult the annual buyer's guides produced by *Automatic Merchandiser* and *Vending Times*. Associations such as the National Automatic Merchandising Association and the International Telecard Association also offer listings of distributors that are members, allowing you to cross-reference your findings and evaluate industry reputation. For contact information on the foregoing, see the Appendix.

Borrowing from Bottlers

For snack and soda types, another way to obtain equipment is to partner with a bottler. "The upside to this strategy is that bottlers provide you with machines for free," notes Donald Blotner of DCB Consulting in Eagan, Minnesota. "The downside is you're limited to selling only that bottler's products."

While the pros and cons may seem apparent, there are hidden dangers. First, vending trends for the foreseeable future clearly indicate those who customize their offerings to their customers' tastes are the ones who will survive. Second, stories of bottlers literally swiping profitable accounts abound.

You'll find countless detailed discussions of the latter issue in both industry periodicals *Automatic Merchandiser* and *Vending Times*, but the important point for those who choose the partnering route is be wary. Partnering remains a viable option at start-up, but successful entrepreneurs move toward owning their own machines with earnest.

Starting from Scratch

If you are a vending innovator, your approach to obtaining machines may be as unique as the specialty you're pursuing. Baltimore pantyhose vending pioneer Janice M. tried following conventional wisdom for locating machines by calling area vending companies. "But they all said, 'No, we've never heard of that.' " Then she consulted *Vending Times* at her local library. "But it didn't have anything listed. It did have different kinds of machines that might have contained pantyhose in them, but nothing that was solely pantyhose vending machines." Undaunted, she tried a patent search. "I called the office of copyrights, patents, and trademarks to ask if anybody had ever [received] a patent for pantyhose vending machines. They told me [that no one had ever] registered."

After doing more research, Janice decided her vision was truly an exception. Figuring she was onto something, she patented the idea herself.

Although the patent protected her brainchild, Janice still lacked the machines necessary to launch her business. So she invented her own. "The father of a girlfriend of mine is a manufacturer," she explains. "He sat down and taught me how to make the machines, how much it would cost, and how long it would take. He helped me design the machines and make some."

For Janice, who describes her wall-mounted units as "slightly larger than a sanitary products machine," a two-column machine costs about $500, a three-column $650. Her largest units, those with four columns, run $750.

Guarding Your Assets

Regardless of your specialty, type of vendors, their age, or where you acquire them, security is always a concern. Protecting machines from vandalism takes various forms.

For food and beverage machines, which spend long hours unsupervised even in upscale lunch rooms, distributor Gumma recommends adding new locks. "Machines are shipped to operators with a shipping lock that everyone in the country has a key for," he reveals. "Bottlers also lend people machines that have the same lock, which means ten different companies in your area could have keys. For about $10 per machine you can have your own lock with your own key.

"We also suggest people with employees use different locks on each route," continues Gumma. "For example, Route A would have a different key from Route B."

Vendor placement also impacts their safety, says Gumma. "For example, if your machines are outside, they should be in view of a cashier, receptionist, or security guard."

Many operators avoid high-risk locations entirely. "I don't do nightclubs," Janice M. declares. "There is too much of a chance people will break into the machines."

Pat W. sticks to convenience stores and small shops where cashiers and clerks can see her telecard vendors. "There are people who place telecard machines in shopping malls, but they really take a lot of abuse. Vandals will do everything from jamming the bill acceptor with a coin to covering them with graffiti."

But the telecard vendor doesn't rely on her customer's security systems completely. "You can't do enough to make your machines safe," Pat W. explains. "Good machines are built so they can be bolted to the floor or the wall and many operators require it. In high-paying locations, I bolt them to the floor using butterfly bolts, which are extra long, and very large washers. When appropriate, I also use chains with locks that are designed to defeat bolt cutters."

"In other locations, I put about 300 pounds of weights in each machine so it's going to take two or three hefty men to get it out the door," she continues. "And, most importantly, I use security locks, which cost between $16 and $45, on the vendors to protect the inventory and cash inside. I buy only well-built machines because a crowbar won't open them quickly or easily."

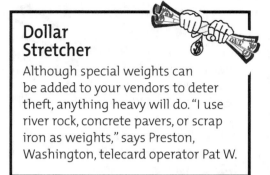

Dollar Stretcher

Although special weights can be added to your vendors to deter theft, anything heavy will do. "I use river rock, concrete pavers, or scrap iron as weights," says Preston, Washington, telecard operator Pat W.

To avoid costly legal battles, make sure your concern for machine safety goes beyond the impact of vandals on your profits. "We advise bolting machines to each other or to a wall," stresses Gumma. "Not so much to reduce damage to the machines, but to keep them from falling on people—which has happened. We show operators how to do this themselves, but many times we'll send a tech out to help."

Good Migrations

Of course, you also need to plan for getting machines from your dock to your clients' locations. "As big as food vending equipment is today, plan to pay someone to move it," says Wayne D. "It'll only cost about $50"—a small price, he points out, compared to a permanent injury of the spine. To find professional movers, look in your Yellow Pages, Wayne recommends.

For smaller equipment, such as telecard vendors, see if you can get help from next door. "I use the guy down the street, a high school kid, or my grandson," Pat W. says. "If they're just moving machines, I pay them $8 an hour. But if they're smart and can figure things out and help me repair things, I pay $12 an hour. It seldom takes less than two hours to travel, work, and come back, but most months I spend well under $50."

Maintenance Matters

Although your only upfront cost will be a basic tool kit and supplies that cost $50 to $100, maintenance and repair will become a routine part of your life as an operator. Therefore, the maintenance and repair training offered by your distributor, as well as the ongoing support policies offered by the manufacturer, bear consideration as you're deciding what to purchase and where to get it.

"I'm not very mechanically inclined, but I learned to be," admits 20-year full-line veteran Wayne D. "If you pay what it costs to have someone else fix your machines, you figure out pretty quickly how to repair it yourself." Most repairs you'll make will

Bright Idea

Bill acceptors give notice they're failing, if you know how to interpret the signs. "Each time you fill a machine, track the number of bills and coins you collect, regardless of denomination," advises Donald Blotner of DCB Consulting in Eagan, Minnesota. "The ratio of bills to coins should be relatively constant, except when a bill acceptor is beginning to fail. Then you'll see a steady increase in the number of coins."

be as simple as clearing jams in the coin mechanism, bill acceptor, or products inside. More serious malfunctions generally require dialing up a professional.

"I don't always have the knowledge to fix a problem, but I call a technician at the manufacturer and ask what to do," says telecard operator Pat W. "They troubleshoot with you over the phone, on-site. None of them have ever said, 'Take it off and send it in.' Every time you can fix something on-site, you not only save money, but your machine's back in service, so you also make money."

Minimize budget-busting repairs to compressors and the like by following the preventive maintenance routine suggested by the manufacturer. "Manufacturer's manuals suggest a routine maintenance for every machine they make," stresses distributor Gumma. "Do operators abide by it? No. Will they lower overhead if they do? Yes."

If you follow specifications, how much maintenance will be required? "We go through preventive maintenance during our training courses and tell operators that high-volume locations will require more maintenance than lower-volume locations," Gumma says. "And we tell people soda and coffee machines have to be adjusted more often."

For a rundown of typical maintenance chores, see "Maintain It Right" on page 89.

Time to Accessorize

Depending on your vending specialty, you'll want to budget for miscellaneous items to deliver power to your vendors, protect electronics from power failures, and clean machines inside and out.

While power cords supplied with your vendors may be adequate, sometimes they are just too short. "You'll definitely need heavy-duty extension cords," advises Pat W. "And put your name on the cords in permanent marker."

Even in the absence of an extension cord, avoid fusing your vendors' circuits by delivering clean, steady current. "Some machines on the market aren't made well enough to block electrical surge," Pat notes. "If a vendor is near a compressor and holiday lights get plugged into the same outlet, or there's other white noise, those certain machines must have a surge protector with a noise filter. They run $20 to $40 at a discount shop. However, there are good-quality machines on the market that have the surge protector and noise filter built into them."

Maintain It Right

Let's face it: The world's a grimy place. Finger oil alone coats every coin and bill in a pocket, wallet, or purse. The air constantly deposits tiny particles on moving and stationary parts. Unless you inherit a fortune, you'll want to fight off your vendor's sworn enemies each week by taking these simple steps:

Clean the coin mechanism and bill acceptor.

- ○ Pour rubbing alcohol on the coin rails, which also cleans the coin acceptor.
- ○ Run a cleaning card through the bill acceptor.
- ○ Swab off bill acceptor belts and sensors.

Check the selection buttons.

- ○ Clean off dirt and check to see if the buttons are making good contact.
- ○ Look on the back side for broken parts or bad connections.

Inspect the selection trays, motors, and spirals.

- ○ Make sure selection trays or shelves sit in their "home" position in the shelf rails.
- ○ Examine all wires going to the motor, tightening any that have loosened.

Check circuit boards.

- ○ Blow dust off boards using a can of compressed air.
- ○ Examine all wires connecting to boards and tighten accordingly.
- ○ Call for support if you see signs of corrosion.
- ○ Reconnect wires properly if you remove any for cleaning or replacement. Improper connections can blow the whole machine.

Inspect the bucket.

- ○ Open the door using minimal force and determine if it's moving freely.
- ○ Examine the hinges and replace when worn.

Clean condenser coils/fins.

- ○ Vacuum off dust with a hand vacuum.
- ○ Remove grease or grime with mild cleanser.

Inspect the power cords.

- ○ Tighten connections between machine cord, extension cord, and wall socket.
- ○ Free pinched wires.
- ○ Replace any cord where the wire's been bared or casing gashed.

Polish the exterior.

- ○ It's a fact: Clean glass and exteriors attract more sales!

Source: Route and Service Driver, *a quarterly companion publication to* Automatic Merchandiser

Other accessories include cleaning cards for cleaning bill acceptors, rubbing alcohol to cleanse coin rails and coin acceptors, glass or multipurpose surface cleaner to swab down fronts, and an appropriate disinfectant to wipe down insides of food and beverage vendors. As mentioned in the previous section, the total cost for a start-up maintenance and repair kit will be $50 to $100.

Which Ones Should I Buy?

Now that you have all the background info, perhaps you're wondering how to decide which machines to buy.

"A start-up operator shouldn't buy equipment before [he or she knows] the location and the requirements of the location," advises Gumma. "Successful operators typically come to us with something already lined up or they've at least got some kind of verbal commitment."

We'll address this issue and much more in Chapter 11. So hold tight for now, and let's move on to another vital consideration—how you're going to get around.

Getting around Town

For many start-up operators, whatever they're currently driving becomes their first route vehicle. "At the time we started, we worked out of the trunk of the car," says Wayne. D., who began with 14 snack, soda, and cigarette machines in five locations. "When we needed a bigger vehicle, we went with a small van."

"I'm using the same car I had prior to starting the business," Janice M. says. "But I'm considering purchasing a small truck next year."

No matter what type of vehicle you choose, remember your insurance company won't cover a loss if you fail to inform them you're using your vehicle for business purposes. Count on your rates increasing when you switch from pleasure to business, but you need look no further than NAMA statistics to know it's worth the investment. Recent vending industry statistics name auto liability the second largest area for both frequency and cost of claims. And remember, you can ease the sting by deducting insurance premiums and other vehicle-related expenses on your income tax return.

> **Beware!**
> Acquiring vendors before clients puts the cart ahead of the horse. "Randomly buying machines and thinking you'll get the right ones is ludicrous," stresses Vince Gumma of American Vending Sales in Chicago. The number of potential customers, male/female mix, ethnicity, age, wages, competitors (convenience stores, superstores, etc.), and even regional preferences impact what's profitable at a given location.

Running on Empty

If your current vehicle won't make the miles, then you must purchase something reliable. Entrepreneurs intending to grow a snack business into a full-time pursuit should head straight for a cargo van. A new one with a sliding door, antilock brakes, air-conditioning, and airbags will cost between $20,000 and $25,000. Like any vehicle, used cargo vans vary in price with age, but plan to pay about $12,000 for a reliable one.

> **Bright Idea**
>
> Whenever you invest in a vehicle for your business, buy from customers or prospects, suggests Hendersonville, Tennessee, full-line operator B.J. S. "We do that whenever we can. When you buy from a customer, it keeps them happy, and hopefully you have a good enough relationship with them that they'll give you a break."

Operators of nonfood vending businesses say it's easy to stay with an automobile. "One of the most important things I've done is have a car that gets good gas mileage," says Pat W. "It's helped me keep my expenses as low as possible."

Buddying Up to Your Back

Lifting items into and out of your vehicle may seem like a no-brainer activity, but your back may disagree. Just as you'll end your vending career early by improperly moving a heavy machine, you can blow out your spine when bending, twisting, reaching, and lifting the products you unload at each location.

This is particularly true if you're operating out of a passenger vehicle because it's not designed for the job. "Utility vans are terrible on your back because you're working on your knees," comments Becky P.

Arguably, your personal mobility is your most important asset as an operator. The best machines in the world won't do you a bit of good if improper lifting lands you in a wheelchair.

Unless you have an uncle who's an orthopedist or your best friend's a chiropractor, a good source of information on proper back care is NAMAs *Be a Buddy to Your Back*. This short video explains the dos and don'ts and comes with a laminated card showing appropriate lifting techniques and six back exercises. For information on how to obtain the video, consult the Appendix.

Stepping Up to Step Vans

As you grow, or if you purchase an operation that's up and running, you'll quickly find yourself upgrading to step vans. A step van is like a bread delivery truck, or a scaled-down version of the ubiquitous brown UPS vehicles.

In addition to expanded capacity and the potential for adding a refrigerated compartment, step vans allow for standing upright inside. This makes them much easier on the back when it comes to lifting chores. Of course the down side is they're pricier than your average cargo van. "By the time we needed a step van, we were a pretty good-sized company," says Wayne D. "We were four or five years old and were grossing over $200,000 annually."

Vending Equipment Expenses

To help you budget, here are furnishing, equipment, and supply costs for the two fictional vending operations we introduced you to in Chapter 6, Quality Snacks and QuickCard.

	Quality Snacks	QuickCard
	New/Used	New/Used
Vendors	$52,500/$26,250	$15,500/$9,300
Vehicle (cargo van)	20,000/12,000	N/A*
Labor (to move machines to locations)	750	240
Security locks (for vendors)	150	200
Surge protector (with noise filter)	N/A	300
Extension cords (heavy-duty)	N/A	100
Safe or lockbox (for vehicle, bolted to floor)	250	100
Dolly (transport inventory/move vendors)	60	60
Cash pouches (zippered, with locks)	50	50
Maintenance and repair kit	100	50
Total Expenditures	**$73,960/$39,460**	**$16,500/$10,300**

*N/A = Not applicable. In other words, this hypothetical operation doesn't own this item.

When you reach the point where a step van is the logical next step, decide which is best to buy the same way you choose vendors, recommends Becky P. "We do research through *Consumer Reports* and get sales pitches from different places. We also go up to people driving certain vehicles and ask them what the pluses and minuses are."

Stop, Thief!

You already know vending is a cash-based business, which means you don't have to hire a receivables department in order to get paid. And your inventory can fit in a vehicle, which means you don't need an expensive location. The flip side of these two facts is you'll be carrying untraceable cash and products around. Protecting these assets requires a pretty simple combination of inexpensive equipment and a little common sense.

Vending Equipment Expenses Worksheet

Here's a handy shopping guide for equipping your business. Although it's designed with the homebased operation in mind, you'll need the same gear if you're in commercial quarters.

For a nifty note sheet, photocopy this page before you begin. Then, when you're finished shopping, total up the costs to give yourself a head start on the "Start-Up Expenses Worksheet" in Chapter 6 on page 58.

Vendors	$
Vehicle	$
Labor (to move machines to locations)	$
Security locks (for vendors)	$
Surge protector (with noise filter)	$
Extension cords (heavy-duty)	$
Safe or lockbox (for vehicle, bolted to floor)	$
Dolly (transport inventory/move vendors)	$
Cash pouches (zippered, with locks)	$
Maintenance and repair kit	$
Total Expenditures	$

Bright Idea

When investing in a safe for your vehicle, consider a punch board instead of a combination lock. Electronic circuits take more time to beat than mechanical devices, increasing your odds of detecting would-be robbers before they make off with your money.

On the equipment side, you'll need a roll-top safe or lockbox that's bolted to the floor in between the seats [of your car, truck or van]," Pat W. reports. "I also carry mace and a cellular phone with me."

Although robberies may be most feared, far more common are thefts due to complacency. We'll talk more about security when we discuss route structures in Chapter 11. But while we're talking about vehicles, now's the perfect time to point out one of the best theft-protection strategies is simply locking your doors.

If you're wondering how you're going to finance all the big-ticket items discussed in this chapter, perhaps you skipped over Chapter 6. (We hope you didn't skip Chapter 6; it's an important one!) If you want to give yourself a head start on your "Start-Up Expenses Worksheet" in Chapter 6, take a look at "Vending Equipment Expenses" on page 92 and fill out the "Vending Equipment Expenses Worksheet" on page 93. Then, when you are wise to the ways of finance, it's time to move on to what you'll put in your vendors. For more on inventory, all you have to do is turn to page 97.

Application for Credit

AMERICAN VENDING SALES INC.

APPLICATION FOR CREDIT

_____ , Applicant

Correct legal name	_____ corporation _____ partnership _____ individual yrs. In business	arcade _____ yes _____ no

Location (street address)	Telephone # ( )

City	State	Zip Code	Federal Tax ID #

Own	Morgagee	Address	City/State/Zip Code	Mortgage balance $	since

Rent	Landlord	Address	City/State/Zip Code	Monthly payment $	since

TRADE REFERENCES

1) Name	Address	City/State/Zip Code	Telephone # ( )

HI credit $	Amount owed $	Length of time doing business	Personal contact

2) Name	Address	City/State/Zip Code	Telephone # ( )

HI credit $	Amount owed $	Length of time doing business	Personal contact

3) Name	Address	City/State/Zip Code	Telephone # ( )

HI credit $	Amount owed $	Length of time doing business	Personal contact

BANK (checking____ Loan____) 1)	Address	City/State/Zip	Personal contact	Account #'s

BANK (checking____ Loan____) 2)	Address	City/State/Zip	Personal contact	Account #'s

INFORMATION ON OFFICERS, PARTNERS, OWNERS

Name	Address	City/State/Zip	S.S. #	Tel. #	Title
Name	Address	City/State/Zip	S.S. #	Tel. #	Title
Name	Address	City/State/Zip	S.S. #	Tel. #	Title

"The undersigned, individually and on behalf of Applicant (if signed as an officer or partner of the corporation or partnership) does hereby certify to the truth, correctness and completeness of the information set forth above and on the reverse side, and understands that American Vending Sales, Inc. will rely upon such information if it decides to extend credit to the undersigned and Applicant. The undersigned and Applicant hereby authorize American Vending Sales, Inc. to investigate all the information provided above, and understand that American Vending Sales, Inc. may contact any or all the parties names. Provided, however, any investigation or contact by American Vending Sales, Inc.shall not be deemed as a waiver of its reliance upon the accuracy of the information provided by the undersigned and Applicant of this Application.

In consideration for any extension of credit by American Vending Sales, Inc. to the undersigned and Applicant, the undersigned, individually and on behalf of Applicant, hereby agrees to the following terms and conditions which shall be deemed applicable to all sales by American Vending Sales, Inc. to the undersigned and/or Applicant.

a) The undersigned and Applicant agree to timely pay all amounts due in connection with any sales made by American Vending Sales, Inc. to the undersigned and/or Applicant;

b) The undersigned and Applicant agree to pay interest upon past due balances at the lesser of two percent per month, or the highest rate of interest permitted by law; and

c) The undersigned and Applicant agree to pay all costs and expenses incurred by American Vending Sales, Inc. in connection with the collection of any balances due from the undersigned and/or Applicant, including by way of description and not limitation, court costs and reasonable attorney's fees."

_____
Signature

Application for Credit, continued

PLEASE COMPLETE THE FOLLOWING AS WELL AS ALL SCHEDULES BELOW:

ASSETS		LIABILITIES	
Cash on hand & in Banks	$ _____	Accts. Payable	$ _____
Accts. & Notes Rec.	_____	Notes payable (sched. B)	_____
Inventories	_____	Unpaid Taxes	_____
Real estate owned (sched. A)	_____	R.E. Mortg. pay (sched. A)	_____
Equipment (net of deprec.)	_____	Other liabilities (please itemize)	_____
Autos & Trucks (NET)	_____	_____	_____
Other assets: (please itemize)	_____	_____	_____
_____	_____		
_____	_____	**Total Liabilities**	$ _____
		Net Worth	$ _____
Total Assets _____	$ _____	**Total Liab. & Net Worth**	$ _____

Net Income–Prior Year Ending _____ / 19 _____ $ _____
                             Mo.   Yr.

Estimated Annual Sales–Current Year Ending _____ / 19 _____ $ _____
                                         Mo.   Yr.

SCHEDULE A–REAL ESTATE OWNED

Property Location	Bank Name	Date Acquired	Original Cost	Original Mortg.	Mortg. Bal.
			$	$	$
			$	$	$
			$	$	$
			$	$	$

SCHEDULE B–NOTES PAYABLE (EQUIPMENT, IMPROVEMENTS, ETC.)

(Bank or Fin. Co.)	Type of Loan	Date of Loan	Amount	(Mo. Pmt.)	(Balance)
			$	$	$
			$	$	$
			$	$	$

In order to induce American Vending Sales, Inc. to enter into sales or extend credit to Applicant, _____ ("Debtor"), the undersigned, being an officer or shareholder of Debtor and/or being financially benefited by the accommodations made by American Vending Sales, Inc., guarantees the full and prompt performance of all of Debtor's present and future contracts, agreements and arrangements with American Vending Sales, Inc. and the full and prompt payment to American Vending Sales, Inc. of any and all sums which may be presently due or declared due and owing to American Vending Sales, Inc. by Debtor or which shall in the future become due or declared due and owing to American Vending Sales, Inc. by Debtor.

This is a continuing Guarantee, and American Vending Sales, Inc. is hereby authorized without notice or demand and without affecting the liability of the undersigned hereunder, from time to time, to (i) extend credit to Debtor, (ii) renew, extend, accelerate or otherwise change the terms of the Debtor's Liabilities, or any instrument, (iii) accept partial payments on Debtor's Liabilities, (iv) and take and hold Collateral for the payment of this Guaranty. American Vending Sales, Inc. may, without notice, assign this Guaranty in whole or in part.

The undersigned waives notice of acceptance of this Guaranty notice of extension of time of payment, notice of any amendments or modification of said agreement and all other notices to which the undersigned might otherwise be entitled by law, and agrees to pay all amounts owing thereafter, upon demand, without requiring any action or proceedings against the debtor.

The undersigned agrees to pay all costs, expenses and attorney's fees incurred in the collection thereof and the enforcement of this Guaranty.

Dated _____ 19 _____

_____

Source: American Vending Sales Inc.

Stocking Your
Machines

Now that we've discussed your automated sales force, let's talk about filling those machines up. While clean, attractive machines invite purchasers to draw near, what's in the machine seals the deal.

"You have to know your market," proclaims Preston, Washington, telecard operator Pat W. "Are they Mexicans? Asians? Europeans? Then you need to find a card, or several cards, to meet the needs of the people in that location. And you need to find cards that have a good discount so that you and your merchant can make a buck."

Product Mix 101

Does this mean you will stock as many different individual items as your total number of columns for all the vendors you own? Hardly. "Your mix will be different for each location," says John Ochi of Vernon Hills, Illinois-based product distributor Five Star Distributors. "But some types of products will be the same in every location."

In addition to determining individual items to stock, satisfying desires for certain categories of products is equally important. According to *Vending Times*, research shows at least 20 percent of consumers will walk away from a machine if they don't find the *kind* of item they want.

In other words, demand does not transfer from one category to another. For example, a person hankering for chewing gum won't buy potato chips, nor will a woman who needs pantyhose settle for knee-high stockings.

Surveying the Landscape

At any given movie theater you'll find tots in line for the animated show and teens queued up for the latest horror flick. Not surprisingly, in the theater called vending, demographics also play a leading role. "We look at the top-selling products in each category and then evaluate the demographics at the location," explains Burnsville, Minnesota, operator Wayne D. "In a facility with truck drivers and blue-collar workers, we don't merchandise the same items as in a location that's heavily female. If it's predominantly female, we offer more low-fat items and diet sodas."

At closed locations, such as offices or factories, pre-surveying the population hones in on preferences even more precisely. "For example, we give our contact at a location a list of beverages and ask them to survey their people," Wayne says. "Then we take the top 8, 10, 16, etc., items, depending on the size of the location, and put those in." But this process often requires some fine-tuning because some survey respondents may not purchase beverages as often as others. "Let's say Diet Coke didn't make the initial cut," illustrates Wayne. "But after we put in the initial inventory, two or three people request Diet Coke. If two or three people buy a Diet Coke every day, then we make a lot of money."

> **⚠ Beware!**
>
> Vendors that stay full between servicings don't mean less work. They mean trouble. "Some guys go into a place, and when they see full machines, say, 'Great, I don't need to stock,'" says Henderson, Tennessee, full-line operator B.J. S. "But if they're not selling, they're not making money."

Open locations require a different approach. "We count on our owners to know their own market," says Pat W., who places telecard vendors in convenience stores. Pat studies regional data and uses the eyeball approach. In her experience, agricultural areas attract seasonal workers of one ethnic background, while naval bases draw another. Observing convenience store customers while she's servicing machines allows Pat to fill in the cracks.

Uncharted Waters

If you go Baltimore pantyhose operator Janice M.'s route and vend a completely new product, trial and error will likely be your guide. "When I started, I only had a two-column machine, so I only had two selections. I did black and white because those are pretty generic colors. Eventually, people started asking if I had other colors. As they would ask me, I would do different selections. I'd think, Maybe I'll do gray and see if that moves—and it did."

While the trial-and-error method may seem confined to new vending specialties, to some extent it's a fact of life in every specialty. "Although our top 10 or 12 snack items will basically be the same in every location, we watch the service frequency of each category, such as chips, candy, or pastry," Wayne D. says. "If the service frequency shows that the pastry isn't selling, then we reduce the pastry spirals at that location and add more chips. You can't just furnish donuts and cookies because [your customers] don't want them every day. And what about the afternoon? In the afternoon they want a cake or a pie."

Variety: The Spice of Life

No matter what you vend, plan to introduce new options often. "It's a penny, nickel, and dime business," stresses Wayne. "Two extra sales a day makes a lot of money at the end of the year. That's what we try to instill in our route people—if you sell $100 more per week just by making changes, you'll take in more money and have a lot of satisfied customers as well."

Why? Your machines may be robots, but your customers aren't. "I know in school we all ate peanut butter and jelly every day," points out Northridge, California, full-line operator Becky P. "But we're not in school. We're dealing with sophisticated adults. So don't get lazy—keep changing your menu."

Freshness Sells

For food-related operators, "Pay attention to the date" is another crucial mantra. "Let's face it, freshness sells," asserts Hendersonville, Tennessee, full-line operator B.J. S. "If there's someone cutting you a deal, you're probably getting close to the expiration date of the product. Most suppliers don't deal on items that are selling well. Nine times out of ten, it's an item that's been sitting around, and somebody's trying to get rid of it."

For full-line operators like B.J., this means the turnaround time between receiving deliveries and placing items in vendors is tight. "Before I purchased the company, we used to stockpile things because the previous owner felt he had to buy more to get a good deal. But if you stockpile, sooner or later your inventory goes bad. Now we turn inventory on a ten-day basis."

In addition to attending to expiration dates, snack and soda operators must compensate for the environment's effect on their chocolate. "You can store it for 48 hours at a time in weather up to 90 degrees without a problem," notes consumables distributor John Ochi. "But some people store it up to 95 degrees."

However, these guidelines mean air temperature—not the climate inside your truck when it's sitting on asphalt in the midsummer sun. For such situations, you can get a simple picnic cooler and pack it with lots of ice. A 64-gallon model with a pull handle and wheels will cost you approximately $50.

Going Cold Turkey

The rules for variety and freshness go double for those in cold food. "You cannot service cold food machines once a week," emphasizes Becky P. "We service the majority of our cold food machines six days a week, and at the very least, every other day. Even if a vendor only needs a few items, and we're just switching things around in the machine, we're working on the machine and we're there."

In addition, cold food sales hinge on eye appeal. "It's basic junior high home economics," says Becky. "Food is visual. Look at the food in the machine. If it doesn't look appealing, get it out of there. What you lose by discarding an item is minimal compared to the

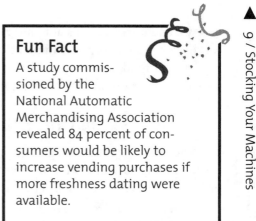

Fun Fact

A study commissioned by the National Automatic Merchandising Association revealed 84 percent of consumers would be likely to increase vending purchases if more freshness dating were available.

overall loss of people coming up and seeing a sandwich that looks nasty. You could have 40 other items that look gorgeous, but that one bad item will destroy the integrity of the entire machine."

Becky also recommends taking time to sit in break rooms. "Watch what people are bringing from home. If you can supply that in the machine, remember, everyone would like to hit that snooze button and not get up and pack a lunch. If they know they can come to work and buy fresh, high-quality food, and the food of their liking, they'd much rather get it there than have to pack a lunch."

With all the extra effort cold food requires, many in the industry will admonish you to avoid it at all costs. But Becky P. says if you're drawn to this specialty there are profits to be made. "You can make money on cold food, but it takes a tremendous amount

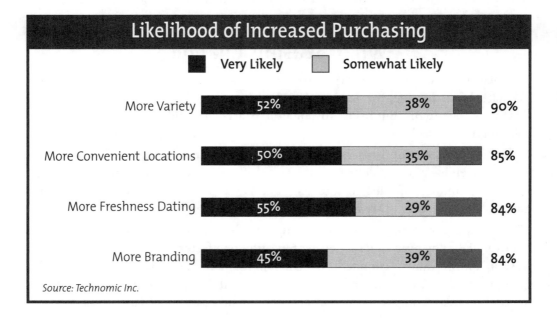

Likelihood of Increased Purchasing

Very Likely ▮ Somewhat Likely ▯

	Very Likely	Somewhat Likely	Total
More Variety	52%	38%	90%
More Convenient Locations	50%	35%	85%
More Freshness Dating	55%	29%	84%
More Branding	45%	39%	84%

Source: Technomic Inc.

of work and a tremendous amount of time," she stresses. "We have 1 percent and less waste, where the industry is 15 percent, because of the way we work it. We totally focus on the cold food, and the rest of the operation takes care of itself—we keep our customers in the room instead of going for the $2.99 fast-food value meal."

Name Brand or Off Brand?

When you begin investigating product options, you will quickly discover most every vending specialty offers a wealth of options. Do you go with recognizable names or less expensive unknowns? The answer depends on your vending line.

"When you're first starting up, stick with the top products your distributor recommends," urges Donald Blotner of Eagan, Minnesota-based DCB Consulting. "Your distributor should know the trends in your immediate area. And it's in his best interest to give you good advice because when you sell, he sells."

On the other hand, when you're vending telecards, what matters most is the amount of talk time for the price. "In the past few years the competition has become really fierce, and there are many more card issuers out there," Pat W. comments. "Once, when I wasn't paying attention for about two months, my sales began going down. [Then I realized] it was because everyone else's rates were going down but mine weren't."

In pantyhose, the story's similar, but in this specialty, quality is key. "I buy my hosiery in bulk and repack them into boxes that fit the machines," explains Janice M. She labels the boxes using standard labels run off on her computer, but there's no indication of the brand that's within. "If I sell a good product at a good price, I get repeat customers," she says.

When Seasons Change

Once you've focused in on your product mix, factor in seasonality before you buy. "When it's hot outside, no one wants to buy pantyhose," remarks Janice. "Instead, they want knee-highs. But from November to March, it's cold, so women switch from knee-highs back to hose."

For telecards it's not the weather itself but the economic trends that follow. "If you are in convenience stores along an interstate that doesn't serve truckers, then sales go up in the summertime due to tourists," Pat W. says. "And no matter where your machines are, Mother's Day is the biggest day of the year."

Food operators report variations throughout the year, but gross sales tend to even out overall. "I don't care if it's a transient location or a factory; machines sell the same, week in and week out," comments Wayne D. "If you have a snowstorm then, yes, it's going to drop. If Christmas falls on a Monday, we'll do more business than if it falls on a Wednesday. And we know that between Thanksgiving and Christmas is one of our lowest points of the year in candy and snacks." But, he says, by studying your business overall, you'll anticipate the anomalies.

B.J. S. concurs. "We have some school business that shuts down in the summer, but we sell more drinks in the summer. In the winter it's more snacks, so it pretty much evens out." He also suggests location diversification helps out. "There's no period that's really slow for us. For example, we have a lot of retail business [such as department stores], so even Christmastime evens out."

Fun Fact

According to a study commissioned by the National Automatic Merchandising Association, 84 percent of consumers surveyed say they would be more likely to increase vending purchases if more brand names were available.

Quantity Questions

With the other variables in front of you, it's time to calculate quantity. Do you fill your machines to the brim or leave some air between product and rim? Obviously, the answer hinges on your research on each location and how often you'll service each machine.

"If it's a gas station/deli in a good traffic area with a two-bin machine, I put in 30 cards of each denomination and check on it every week," says Pat W. "If it doesn't sell any more than ten of the $10 denominations, then I'd let the $10 inventory run down and only keep $15 denominations in there from week to week."

On the other hand, operators with less expensive inventory tend to fill each machine to the brim. "Generally, I fill my machines completely," reports Janice M., who dedicates her Saturdays to filling machines. "That generally gives me about a two- to three-week time span before I have to come back and fill them up again."

Regardless of the type and quantity you choose, remember to figure your first refill into your start-up costs. "The first time you refill a machine, you must have more inventory," comments Pat. "If you've got, say, $1,000 in cards, shipping fees, and taxes for a machine, the first time you go in to collect money, you need to have purchased that many cards to fill the machine at the same time you take the money out. So you actually have a start-up cost of not $1,000 but $2,000 because you have to fill that machine back up before you have the money out of the machine to buy more cards."

For some examples of beginning inventory and ballpark costs for one of our hypothetical vending businesses, see the "Start-Up Inventory Expenses" form on page 114. Then use the worksheet on page 116 to figure your own start-up inventory expenses.

Priced to Sell

Before we move on to discussing where to purchase your inventory, a few words about pricing are in order. Virtually every other retail business is your competitor.

Smart Tip

Tip...

Some types of vending are subject to surges in demand. "If a convention comes in or some seasonal workers arrive unexpectedly, one person can come in and buy $200 worth of cards," explains Preston, Washington, telecard operator Pat W. To meet such spikes, she works closely with her clients. "I tell them 'Just call me if you run out.'"

Therefore, unlike businesses that offer a service, such as consulting, your pricing process requires less guesswork.

While consumers expect to pay for the convenience a vending machine offers, their generosity only goes so far. One way to determine going rates is to survey your competitors' vendors. In established vending specialties, such as snacks and sodas, industry figures show your goods will cost 50 percent of the sales price. In other words, if a candy bar costs you 35 cents, a consumer will pay about 70 cents.

For a completely new form of vending, such as pantyhose, doing your own research will help you establish the right price. "When I found out what others charged, I just marked mine up about 50 to 75 cents—in some cases $1—because of the location," says Janice M. of her original pricing strategy. Now she purchases her inventory in bulk, which lowers her cost to about 30 percent of gross sales.

"Depending on the location, the price generally ranges between $2 and $4," Janice says. "It's not outrageous because I do still want people to continue to come back. So you don't want to scare them away by charging them $5 for something they could get for $3. But at the same time, you don't want people to think you're stupid and only charge $3 when you really should be charging $5. And customers know that. Most customers expect to pay a little bit more, especially getting them from a vending machine. And they're usually quite surprised that I don't charge more for the product. But I do charge enough to make a profit and cover my costs."

With telecards, the pricing system works in reverse because the consumer's price is fixed. Currently, cards come in denominations of $5, $10, and $20. Your cost hinges on the card issuer. "Cards vary a lot, from 22 to 42 percent discount from retail," notes Pat W. "It depends on the card issuer, the kind of card they're selling, and what market they're targeting, such as Asian, Mexican, or domestic."

Bargain Basement

While it's tempting to set your prices lower than the average to attract new clients, successful operators stress running the numbers or you'll run in the red. "I've been at the cash and carries with the guys that are just one-person operations running out of their van, and they're crying in their milk," Becky P. observes. "And I say to them, 'What are you charging? What are you paying for that product?' I can't tell you how many of them could not tell me what their unit cost was.

"Then I pull out a piece of scratch paper," she continues. "I say, 'Look, you're charging 50 cents for a candy bar and it's costing you 32 cents. It's costing you 8.25 percent sales tax and 10 percent commission. What do you have left? What are you doing here? You need to charge 60 cents, and you need to educate your customer on why you need to charge 60 cents.' "

Paying Your Client's Commission

Many operators take location commission into consideration when establishing price. "If we don't pay commission, then it's one price; otherwise it's another," comments B.J. S.

Which begs the question, why commission at all? The answer: Your competitors may offer commissions, which means clients will expect it. Although clients don't depend on commissions to balance the books, they do use them to fund incidentals such as holiday parties, birthday or illness cards and flowers, productivity rewards such as dinner certificates, etc.

Commissions vary from location to location and by vending specialty. For food operators with gross sales less than $1 million, commissions average out to about 5

It's a Planogram!

Operators with a wide variety of items in each machine, particularly food vendors, are turning to a formal way of determining what and how much to buy.

Called "planogramming," the basic idea is making a simple line drawing (like a tic-tac-toe grid, only bigger) of each of your vendors. Then, inside each cell of the grid, note where you intend to place products in a given machine.

Creating a planogram, or map, for each vendor gives you a visual representation of what your customers will see and allows you to make adjustments before you spend hours filling machines to the brim. In addition, planogramming assists you with matching location survey data to machine columns, helps you identify product trends, allows you to purchase inventory more cost-efficiently, etc.

Planogramming is part of the big-picture process of optimizing sales. Sales optimization is known in the industry as category management.

We'll delve into planogramming and category management in more detail when we discuss product merchandising in Chapter 13. For now, it's enough for you to know that maximizing sales goes beyond simply purchasing the right inventory.

percent of gross, according to National Automatic Merchandising Association statistics. For food operators with gross sales of more than $1 million, commissions average about 10 percent.

On the other hand, telecard operator Pat W. reports paying commissions averaging 20 percent, while pantyhose operator Janice M. notes her commissions average about 12.5 percent.

Sourcing Resources

As you're getting up to speed on inventory issues, it's important to know where to buy your consumables. Just like any other retail business, your supplier options range from manufacturers to wholesale warehouse clubs and fall into the following basic categories:

- *Manufacturers*. Producers of goods, manufacturers often sell directly to operators in nonfood vending specialties such as pantyhose or telecards. In food vending circles, you're more likely to purchase from any of the other supply sources until you become large enough to warehouse products yourself. However, manufacturer's sales representatives may call on you to tell you about their products, purchasing incentives, and/or consumer promotions.

- *Brokers*. Another term for brokers is "independent sales representatives." Brokers represent manufacturers that are too small to—or choose not to—maintain their own internal sales forces. They may work for a number of different manufacturers but generally don't represent manufacturers of competing products such as Snickers and Nestlé's Crunch candy bars. Like manufacturer's representatives, brokers inform you about product offerings, offer purchasing incentives, and clue you in to special consumer promotions. However, brokers neither produce goods nor warehouse them. If you're a large vending operation, you'll receive products you buy from your broker through the manufacturer or a local distributor. If you're a small operation, you'll pick the products up from the distributor yourself.

- *Distributors*. Warehousers and sellers of goods, distributors rarely maintain sales forces that call on operators. Instead, distributors either deliver goods sold to you by manufacturers and brokers or allow you to purchase from them directly, passing on purchasing incentives and alerting you to consumer promotions. Many distributors also offer cash and carry services, as described below.

- *Cash and carries*. This is the industry term for warehouse clubs such as Sam's Club and Costco. The main difference between a distributor and a warehouse club is minimum quantity. Distributors generally require purchasing by the case while warehouse clubs permit purchasing as little as one bag of chips if you so desire. Because they allow single-item purchases, the cost of goods at warehouse clubs tends to fall between distributor and retail. While cash and carry once applied only to warehouse clubs, distributors are now establishing cash and carry services to compete with warehouse clubs for smaller accounts.

- *Commissary.* Commissaries prepare and sell sandwiches, salads, and other fresh refrigerated foods. In the past, when a vending operation grew very large, an in-house commissary was established. Today many large operators still support in-house commissaries, but the trend is toward outsourcing to reduce the myriad costs associated with fresh food handling and preparation.

> ⚠️ **Beware!**
> An incomplete understanding of your specialty's commission structure can spell disaster. During start-up, Wayne D. lost one-third of his business after reducing the commission on an account. "I didn't have a complete understanding of how the beverage business worked," says the Burnsville, Minnesota, full-line operator. "The bottler came in and took the account away from me."

To locate suppliers in your specialty area, consult the annual buyer's guides produced by *Automatic Merchandiser* and *Vending Times* magazines. Associations such as NAMA and the ITA also offer listings of suppliers who are members, allowing you to cross-reference your findings and evaluate industry reputation. For contact information on the forgoing, see the Appendix.

The Broker Connection

At first glance, it may seem a start-up's best bet for purchasing inventory is a distributor. Certainly, distributors offer an array of advantages, but astute vending operators know brokers perform a vital industry role. According to Jim Patterson of Patterson Co. Inc. in Kenilworth, Illinois, brokers evaluate the available manufacturers and products before selecting the ones they represent. "Brokers can give you supporting reasons why a particular brand is better or who it appeals to, such as a consumer who wants more quantity than quality." In addition, a good broker knows consumer purchasing trends and can advise you when to reduce your salty snacks in favor of more pastries. "Because we handle multiple brands, we recognize trends," Patterson says. "We see things moving back and forth within categories and between categories."

A broker also provides marketing and merchandising support. "We provide static clings to put on your machines that promote a consumer contest, particular brand, or concept such as value meal," asserts Patterson, a member of the National Vending Brokers Association. "For example, [some campaigns promote] the concept of purchasing a sandwich and a beverage as a way to compete with the fast-food chains."

Distributor Distinction

While a distributor will inform you of consumer promotions and purchasing programs, such as rebates, you will have to do the legwork yourself. On the other hand, distributors don't have a vested interest in particular products. Instead, their motivation is helping you boost sales, regardless of the brand or manufacturer.

"Most distributors have a monthly price book containing every product they carry," says John Ochi of Five Star Distributors. "It's a catalog, ordering guide, and inventory-monitoring tool all in one. We try to make purchasing as efficient and brainless as possible."

As a start-up operator, you should expect precise information and advice from distributors on the types and quantities to stock in your machines, Ochi says. This takes the guesswork out of initial inventory purchases and jump-starts your sales by ensuring you offer what's most desirable to consumers in a given area at a given time.

A superior distributor also provides ongoing support. "First and foremost, you should expect a good distributor to be a conduit of information," Ochi notes. Distributors know local purchasing trends, monitor industry issues, and answer just about any question you might have.

In addition, quality distributors even track operator purchases and report statistical information to manufacturers, according to Ochi. "Then, the manufacturers have data that they can translate into purchasing programs specific to regional consumer preferences."

Finally, expect your distributor to extend credit. "Assuming you have an open credit background, you should expect to get credit," Ochi says. "If your history's not good, you'll have to earn credit."

Take a peek at the "Application for Credit" on page 112 to find out what kind of information suppliers want before they'll give you credit. For an example of a distributor's monthly price book, turn to page 109.

Credit Where Credit Is Due

This brings us to a more general discussion of credit in the vending industry. As in the case of food distributors, some suppliers will extend you credit based on your history, and some will require you to build a positive payment history with them.

In other cases, such as telecards, credit is more difficult to come by. "Card issuers seldom give credit to start-ups," Pat W. notes. "They want you to buy from them for

Distributor's Monthly Price Book

SEPTEMBER 1999

Item Description	Case Wt / Pack	Unit Wt	Promo Incl.	BKT 1 Price	Unit	Volume Discount Qty	Price/Each	Item #	Wk1 Wk2 Wk3 Wk4
NABISCO									
Air Crisps Cheese Nips	7 1 / 48 / 1.75 oz			14.65	0.305	10	14.36 0.299	06819	
Air Crisps Original	8 1 / 48 / 2.00 oz			14.65	0.305	10	14.36 0.299	06829	
Air Crisps Sour Cream & Onion	8 1 / 48 / 2.00 oz			14.65	0.305	10	14.36 0.299	06830	
Nabisco Cheese Nips	8 1 / 60 / 1.65 oz			16.16	0.269	10	15.84 0.264	06802	
Ritz Bits Cheese Crackers	7 1 / 60 / 1.75 oz			16.27	0.271	10	15.94 0.266	06804	
Ritz Bits Peanut Butter Crackers	7 1 / 60 / 1.75 oz			16.27	0.271	10	15.94 0.266	06803	
Ritz Crackers 2-Pack	5 1 / 300 / 0.00 oz			19.27	0.064	10	18.90 0.063	01658	
Ritz Snack Mix 1.5 Oz	6 1 / 60 / 1.50 oz			16.14	0.269	10	15.82 0.264	07144	
Saltines 2-Pack	6 1 / 300 / 0.00 oz			7.46	0.025	10	7.31 0.024	01518	
Saltines 2-Pack	8 1 / 500 / 0.00 oz			9.80	0.020	10	9.61 0.019	01666	
Wheat Thins	8 1 / 60 / 1.75 oz			16.16	0.269	10	15.84 0.264	006801	
Chips Ahoy Snack Size	9 1 / 60 / 2.00 oz			14.52	0.242	10	14.23 0.237	01548	
Fig Newtons	18 1 / 120 / 2.20 oz			30.00	0.250	10	29.40 0.245	01579	
Fig Newtons - Fat Free	9 1 / 60 / 2.10 oz			16.48	0.275	10	16.15 0.269	01525	
Lorna Doone Shortbread Cookies	13 1 / 120 / 1.50 oz			26.52	0.221	10	25.99 0.217	01544	
Nutter Butter Tray Cookies	9 1 / 60 / 1.90 oz			17.10	0.285	10	16.76 0.279	06812	
Oreo Cookies	15 1 / 120 / 1.80 oz			26.52	0.221	10	25.99 0.217	01546	
Snackwells Chocolate Cookies	8 1 / 60 / 1.70 oz			17.09	0.285	10	16.75 0.279	06821	
Snackwells Creme Cookies	8 1 / 60 / 1.70 oz			16.55	0.276	10	16.21 0.270	06820	
Snackwells Red Fat Choc Chip Cookie	7 1 / 60 / 1.50 oz			17.09	0.285	10	16.75 0.279	06822	
Swiss Creme Cookies	15 1 / 120 / 1.80 oz			27.40	0.228	10	26.85 0.224	01547	
Vanilla Wafers Bag Cookies	9 1 / 60 / 2.00 oz			16.16	0.269	10	15.84 0.264	01583	
Planters Dry Roasted Peanuts	12 1 / 144 / 1.75 oz		1.44	33.22	0.231	10	32.53 0.226	07697	
Planters Honey Roasted Peanuts	10 1 / 144 / 1.00 oz		1.44	23.12	0.161	10	22.63 0.157	07696	
Planters Hot Spicy Peanuts	17 1 / 144 / 1.75 oz		1.44	33.22	0.231	10	32.53 0.226	07700	
Planters Peanut Bar	16 3 / 48 / 1.60 oz			38.80	0.269	10	38.02 0.264	07172	
Planters Peanuts	10 1 / 144 / 1.00 oz		1.44	21.67	0.150	10	21.21 0.147	07692	
Planters Peanuts 1.75 Oz	12 1 / 144 / 1.75 oz		1.44	33.22	0.231	10	32.53 0.226	07698	
Planters Pnt Btr Square Chse Crkrs	12 1 / 120 / 1.40 oz			17.44	0.145	10	17.09 0.142	07512	
Planters Potato Stix	5 1 / 60 / 1.00 oz			12.43	0.207	10	12.18 0.203	07136	
* Gummi-Saver 5 Flavor	27 10 / 24 / 1.50 oz			74.60	0.311	10	73.11 0.305	80300	
* Lifesavers Intense Fruit Chews	48 12 / 24 / 2.06 oz			94.66	0.329	10	92.77 0.322	55600	
* Now & Later Classic	26 6 / 24 / 2.52 oz			48.88	0.339	10	47.90 0.333	55010	
* Now & Later Radberry	26 6 / 24 / 2.52 oz			48.88	0.339	10	47.90 0.333	55020	
NESTLE FOOD									
* Baby Ruth 288 Ct	42 8 / 36 / 2.10 oz			94.49	0.328			33481	
* Butterfinger 288 Ct	42 8 / 36 / 2.10 oz			94.49	0.328			44102	
* Nestle Butterfinger BB's	34 8 / 36 / 1.70 oz		2.88	91.62	0.318			21888	
* Oh Henry 288 Ct	37 8 / 36 / 1.80 oz			94.49	0.328			08817	
* Raisinets 288 Ct	29 8 / 36 / 1.38 oz			94.49	0.328			08954	
* Butterfinger	31 4 / 48 / 2.10 oz			62.99	0.328			3320	
* Crunch	21 4 / 48 / 1.55 oz			62.99	0.328			13760	
* 100 Grand 10% More	34 8 / 36 / 1.65 oz			94.49	0.328			035112	
* 100 Grand Bar	16 4 / 36 / 1.50 oz			47.39	0.329			2079	
* Oh Henry	19 4 / 36 / 1.80 oz			47.39	0.329			891	

* Denotes items sold by the box

Source: Five Star Distributors Inc.

Smart Tip

Tip...

You want to make sure you don't just look for the best rates. Make sure you're dealing with reliable people who have been in the industry for a long time.

a year or so first." Until you are extended credit, your options typically are cash on delivery (c.o.d.) or paying by credit card.

Once you receive credit, expect to be granted what's typically referred to as either "30 days net" or "net 30," for short. "With one of my hosiery suppliers, I can pay half down, and they finance the rest for 30 days," reports Janice M. "And I have one company where I just order my stuff, they ship it to me, and I pay it in 30 days. Sometimes I'm a few days late, and sometimes I'm a few days early, so it works both ways."

Purchasing Pitfalls

Although most operators purchase from brokers, for distributors or cash and carries, going straight to the source pays dividends for some specialties. "The competition has become really fierce," says telecard operator Pat W. "There are many card issuers and brokers now. Yesterday I found two I'd never heard of before. And they're offering fantastic rates."

Although she could purchase through a broker, Pat W. advocates doing the research yourself. "You want to make sure you don't just look for the best rates. Make sure you're dealing with reliable people who have been in the industry for a long time. I've seen issuers that have taken out four-color ads and have gone under."

The danger with telecard issuers is that anyone can purchase a block of time from a long-distance company and begin selling cards. Then, the unscrupulous simply fail to pay the bill, change the name of their business, and move on. Eventually, the long-distance company voids the cards, leaving purchasers in the lurch.

Simply sticking with big-name telephone companies isn't entirely the answer either, stresses the retiree who watched one of the giants discontinue issuing cards with no fanfare. Although this company honored cards already purchased, its abrupt departure disrupted operators who relied on them.

Your Network for Success

Regardless of your inventory source, building good supplier relations is one of the keys to

Beware!

For some in emerging vending specialties, ongoing research is key. "It's not like you get your knowledge and then go to work for four or five years," Preston, Washington, telecard operator Pat W. emphasizes. "The industry is changing all the time. You have to keep reading the industry publications, talking to industry associations, and networking with other operators."

success. "If you don't [establish good relationships], chances are you're going to be an island unto yourself," warns Five Star Distributors' Ochi. "You're going to make a lot of mistakes, and it's less likely you'll succeed."

"Your relationship with your suppliers and your banker is just as important as with your customers," echoes full-line operator Becky P. "It's so important to have relationships with everybody because they will back you up. For instance, when it's 105 degrees outside and you are out of cups for your cold beverage machines, [you want to count on] your distributor to drive clear across town to bring you cups. Your distributor wants you to succeed. Because when you succeed, then they succeed, too." Keep the lines of communication open between you and your distributors and your business will thrive.

▲

Application for Credit

A-1 Vending Machines

000 Fairway Ave.
Vernon Hills, IL 60000
Phone: (000) 555-9900 Fax: (000) 555-9910

STANDARD CREDIT TERMS

Name of firm or individual _____

Address _____

City_____State _____Zip _____

Phone _____

Years in business _____

hereby applies for credit in accordance with terms and conditions of Five Star Dist. Inc, Vernon Hills, IL credit policies. The following information must be provided. It will be held in the strictest confidence.

❏ Corporation   ❏ Incorporated in the last 12 months

❏ Partnership   ❏ Individual

Name(s) of principal(s) _____

Address _____

City_____State _____Zip _____

Phone _____

Bank _____

Bank address_____

City_____State _____Zip _____

Bank officer or department _____

Application for Credit, continued

References (please fill out with full address):

1. _____

_____

2. _____

_____

3. _____

_____

❑ Check here if cash sales are okay until credit is approved.

Is it your company's intent to cash discount?   ❑Yes   ❑No

We certify that all the information on this form is correct. We fully understand your credit terms and agree to the proper payment in consideration of extended credit.

Signed _____

Title _____ Date _____

If Five Star Distributors engages the services of an attorney in the collection of any overdue accounts, the payment of reasonable attorney fees attributable therto shall become an obligation of the Customer of Five Star Distributions to the extent permitted by the law

PLEASE DO NOT WRITE BELOW THIS LINE

Reference checked by _____

Credit approved by _____

Reference results _____

Credit refused by _____ Date _____

Source: Five Star Distributors Inc.

Quality Snacks Start-Up Inventory Expenses

To help you budget, here is a sample inventory list and product cost for Quality Snacks, the fictional snack vending operation we introduced in Chapter 6. Quality owns 15 snack vendors, which, for ease of illustration, are considered to be all of the same configuration and offer the same products.

Inventory Type	Approximate Unit Cost	Unit Count Per Vendor	Approximate Cost Per Vendor	Cost for 15 Vendors*
ROW #1—LARGE SINGLE-SERVING SALTY SNACKS				
Snyders Olde Tyme Pretzels	0.267	8	$2.14	$32.10
Fritos corn chips	0.292	8	2.34	35.10
Cheetos	0.292	8	2.34	35.10
Doritos nacho tortilla chips	0.292	8	2.34	35.10
Cheese & Bacon Tato Skins	0.267	8	2.14	32.10
ROW #2—SALTY SNACKS				
Sunshine Cheez—Regular Flavor	0.180	10	1.80	27.00
Jays Oke Doke Cheese Popcorn	0.160	10	1.60	24.00
Jays Regular Potato Chips	0.160	10	1.60	24.00
Jays Open Pit BBQ Potato Chips	0.160	10	1.60	24.00
Snyders Mini Pretzels	0.163	10	1.63	24.45
ROW #3—COOKIES/CRACKERS/SNACKS				
Ritz Bits Cheese Crackers	0.283	10	2.83	42.45
Austin Zoo Animal Cracker Cookies	0.180	10	1.80	27.00
Knott's Berry Farm Raspberry Cookies	0.222	10	2.22	33.30
Kellogg's Rice Krispies Treats	0.350	10	3.50	52.50
Famous Amos Chocolate Chip Cookies	0.250	10	2.50	37.50
ROW #4—CANDY/SNACK BARS				
Snickers	0.344	18	6.19	92.85
Starburst	0.344	18	6.19	92.85
Reese's Peanut Butter Cups	0.344	18	6.19	92.85
Planter's Peanuts	0.208	18	3.74	56.10
Butterfinger	0.344	18	6.19	92.85
Kit Kat	0.344	18	6.19	92.85
Oreo Cookies	0.233	18	4.19	62.85
Twix	0.344	18	6.19	92.85
Twizzlers	0.344	18	6.19	92.85
NutRageous	0.344	18	6.19	92.85

Quality Snacks Start-Up Inventory Expenses, continued

Inventory Type	Approximate Unit Cost	Unit Count Per Vendor	Approximate Cost Per Vendor	Cost for 15 Vendors*
ROW #5—CANDY/SNACK BARS				
M&M's Peanut	0.344	18	6.19	92.85
PayDay	0.344	18	6.19	92.85
Milky Way	0.344	18	6.19	92.85
Baby Ruth	0.344	18	6.19	92.85
ReeseSticks	0.344	18	6.19	92.85
3 Musketeers	0.344	18	6.19	92.85
Tootsie Roll twin pack	0.306	18	5.51	82.65
Hershey Almond	0.344	24	8.26	123.90
Nestlé Crunch	0.344	24	8.26	123.90
ROW #6—PASTRIES				
Kellogg's Pop Tarts Sugar Cinnamon	0.361	12	4.33	64.95
Kellogg's Pop Tarts Frosted Strawberry	0.361	12	4.33	64.95
Cloverhill Big Texas Cinnamon Roll	0.391	12	4.69	70.35
Plantation Olde New England Brownie	0.323	12	3.88	58.20
Cloverhill Baking Jumbo Chocolate Donut	0.392	12	4.70	70.50
ROW #7—GUM & MINTS				
Wrigley's Doublemint gum	0.175	20	3.50	52.50
Wrigley's Juicy Fruit gum	0.175	20	3.50	52.50
Carefree bubble gum	0.200	20	4.00	60.00
Life Savers Five Flavor	0.240	20	4.80	72.00
Life Savers Pep-O-Mint	0.240	20	4.80	72.00
Cost of Beginning Inventory				**$2,872.95**
Cost of First Refill (each vendor one-half full)**				**$1,436.48**
Total Start-Up Inventory Cost				**$4,309.43**

Minimum purchase is one case.

**Suggested servicing is at half-full to avoid empties. See Chapter 12 for more information.

Source: Five Star Distributors Inc.

Start-Up Inventory Expenses Worksheet

Here's a handy guide for figuring your start-up inventory costs. For a nifty note sheet, photocopy this page before you begin. To adapt the worksheet for businesses with vendors that hold different amounts of product, use one sheet per vendor and a final sheet to tally it all up. Then, when you're finished, total up the costs to give yourself a head start on the "Start-Up Expenses Worksheet" in Chapter 6 on page 58.

Inventory Type	Unit Cost	Number of Units	Inventory Cost
Cost of Beginning Inventory			
Cost of First Refill			
Total Start-Up Inventory Cost			

Hired
Hands

If you're planning to launch into vending solo, you're in good company. Industry estimates say as many as one-third of all vending businesses are one-person bands.

However, few businesses, regardless of their industry, go it alone over their entire life span. Whether you remain a one-person entity or grow large enough to take on employees, at some point you'll need a little help from your friends.

A Family Affair

Many vending entrepreneurs follow the time-honored tradition of involving their families in the day-to-day operation of their businesses. This not only supplies the business with low-overhead labor but also helps the family unit hang together through the inevitable three to five years of long hours any entrepreneurial effort requires.

"Although it's not essential, it's a great help to have your family involved," points out Burnsville, Minnesota, full-line operator Wayne D. "Especially if your object is to build up to being a full-time business—if it's part of you, it's part of them."

Like many all-in-the-family outfits, Wayne's wife and son have assisted with filling machines, answering trouble calls, and keeping the books. Involving his family even allowed him to act on a growth opportunity only a year after starting the business. "We bought a small route that was a spin-off of a larger vending company's routes," he explains. "My son was in high school at that time, and he serviced the route two or three evenings a week."

While Wayne's situation is typical, you don't need a traditional family unit or older children to pull it off. A single mother of three children, Baltimore operator Janice M. takes her children along for her Saturday filling routine. "I have a 6- and a 7-year-old. They know how to fill those machines up just as well as I do. They'll go right in the bathroom with me, put a chair under the machine, and start putting the boxes in themselves."

Acquaintance Assistants

Preston, Washington, telecard operator and retiree Pat W. uses both family members and neighbors interested in picking up a little cash. For Pat, installing new machines and moving existing ones to new locations are the chores where assistance is required. "I can't lift anything much over 25 pounds, so I've always had someone help me install machines," she says. Her helpers range from high school students to the hardware hank up the block. If they only move machines, Pat compensates them at a rate of $8 per hour for a minimum of two hours. However, those

> **Fun Fact**
> Between one-quarter and one-third of all vending companies are one-man or one-woman businesses, according to *Vending for Investors,* by longtime industry guru G. Richard Schreiber, respected professor, prolific author, and president emeritus of the National Automatic Merchandising Association.

who also help set up new machines, test their operability on-site, or repair recalcitrant units receive $12 per hour. "The most I've paid [for help] in a month is $300," asserts Pat. "That's when I've had a whole bunch of machines come in."

Pat's expenditures on assistants usually average well under $50 per month, and she hires all workers on an independent contractor basis. "I've never paid more than $600 to any one person in any one year," Pat comments, referring to the threshold for reporting payments to independent contractors to the IRS.

Because her pantyhose machines must be mounted on clients' walls, Janice M. uses a temp agency to ensure experienced individuals mount her machines. The charge for these workers runs about $13 per hour. "Although it generally takes only two hours, I usually have to pay a minimum of four hours," she says. "But I don't mind paying for four hours because the quality of the workmanship is better."

Retraining Programs: A Good Source

Another approach to acquiring qualified help is seeking out government retraining programs. In addition to tax incentives for hiring so-called "disadvantaged workers," Janice M. discovered this avenue offers monetary and retention rewards.

"Through the welfare-to-work program, they pay me to train people, and they pay the people a wage during training," she says. "In return, I have to hire the people I train, with health benefits, and they have to work for me for a year. Since I have to train people anyway, I might as well get paid. And it guarantees me a worker for a year, which is great."

The pantyhose vendor also looks at the program as an investment in marketing. "Most of these people have never had a job before, so it's good to have [working for me] on their resumes. And it's good for me to be on their resumes."

Ready for a Route Driver

For most vending operators, the first true employee is a route driver. Although the term implies someone who simply transports items from one place to another, a vending route driver does everything short of accounting, marketing, and major repairs. Route drivers assist with purchasing at cash and carries, load their own inventory, decide on product rotation at locations, fill machines, conduct preventive maintenance, and handle routine trouble calls.

At what point you'll need regular assistance varies. While pantyhose vendor Janice M. grosses less than $10,000 per year and works at another job part time, she employs two part-timers on an occasional basis.

For food operators, the most likely scenarios are growing into or purchasing an operation with several hundred thousand in gross sales. "At around $300,000 gross, annually, you'll need a route driver or maybe a half-time route driver," according to Donald Blotner of DCB Consulting in Eagan, Minnesota.

Northridge, California, full-line operator Becky P. concurs. "We had no employees our first five years, and we were growing the whole time. But there gets to be a point when there's just no way. You get to a certain volume, and you require support.

"Today, our theory is, to support a truck, it has to do $5,000 to $6,000 per week in gross sales," she continues. "So when a truck gets to $7,000 or $8,000 a week, then it's time to start thinking about getting another truck and more employees," says the full-line operator, who takes the unusual approach of employing two people for every truck.

"We run two to a vehicle for safety, morale, and service," explains the Los Angeles-area operator. "In one hour, they can do two hours' worth of servicing at a single location. While one driver is filling a machine, the other one cleans and repairs malfunctioning equipment."

The Right Stuff

To find employees, successful operators use the standard tactics of placing newspaper ads. "We choose not to recruit or hire from other vending companies," says Wayne D. "We feel they bring too many bad habits—they don't want to do things our way; they want to do things their way."

While many operators voice similar opinions, not everyone agrees. "We put up fliers at the cash and carries," notes Becky P. "Guys who come to us from other companies tell us other people train for one to two weeks. We have intensive training for 90 days. We will not turn them loose for 90 days. We tell them upfront we're going to break all their old habits, that this is a philosophy that you've never heard before. But it works for us, and this is the way you're going to do it."

Wherever you look for employees, remember they're on the front lines. No longer will you be interacting with clients and customers at the locations you pass off. Instead, your workers will be representing you and your company. This means you're placing your business reputation (your most valuable asset) into their hands.

"You need more than just a body capable of carrying around products and placing them in the right slot," emphasizes Blotner. "They must be just as hard-working, outgoing, and customer service-oriented as you are. And they must show an interest in merchandising products to

> **Tip...**
>
> **Smart Tip**
> Save time and energy on training new employees by evaluating performance immediately. "You can see the overall attitude in the first few weeks," says Hendersonville, Tennessee, full-line operator B.J. S. "I can't remember the last time I was surprised by a person after the first three months."

encourage sales, as well as a fundamental under-standing of the financial realities of the vend-ing industry. In other words, consider what makes a successful vending operator, and apply the same yardstick to those you hire."

For Hendersonville, Tennessee, full-line operator B.J. S., this means taking the H. Ross Perot approach. "When he hires people, he sits down, looks them in the eye, and says, 'Is this a guy I would want to sit in a foxhole with.' I use the same approach. If I don't think the chemistry is there, I don't bother."

Vending-specific employee materials can be obtained from the National Automatic Merchandising Association using the contact information listed in the Appendix.

Smart Tip
You don't have to rein-vent the wheel when establish-ing hiring guidelines, training procedures, and employee poli-cies. Industry associations such as the National Automatic Merchandising Association, (312) 346-0370, offer industry-specific publications and train-ing tools to help new employers succeed.

Breaking Them In

Whether you hire old hands or fresh faces, the bulk of employee education is typ-ically done in the field. "All of our training is hands-on," states B.J. S. "A supervisor rides along with them for a couple of weeks. After that, they let them go for a couple of days and then send someone along with them again to see how they're doing."

While informal training is the historical norm, vending, like many industries, is beginning to realize the competitive advantages of more formal instruction. "There's formal training that's evolving now," says John Ochi of Vernon Hills, Illinois-based Five Star Distributors. "Specific product manufacturers, such as Nabisco, are developing formal training programs and materials to help operators and their employees improve their product merchandising."

Recently, articles devoted to the value of training abound in industry publications such as *Automatic Merchandiser* and *Vending Times* magazines. NAMA's forward-looking Hudson report also emphasizes increasing the amount and sophistication of training to remain competitive. "The business environment surrounding the vending and food-services industry will be faster-paced, more complex, and more challenging in every respect than in the past," the Hudson report says. "The key to competitive advantage in any field is to have a superior team of managers and employees. Invest in your organization's human capital—educate and train your people."

Paying a Fair Wage

However you locate and train employees, compensation will be the first thing on their minds. If you're wondering what's fair, NAMA's *Wage Rates and Benefits Survey* can be your guide. Updated regularly, the manual breaks down wages and benefits by job function and by region, making quick work of knowing what your competitors are offering.

But successful operators advise going beyond your local average. "We compensate above industry standards because we want a quality person," Wayne D. emphasizes. "That's been one of the problems with the industry as a whole—it's been noted as low-pay."

To get quality work, Janice M. recommends paying even occasional employees a reasonable rate. "There's a high school student I pay $6.50 an hour because that's minimum wage. I pay my adult worker $10 an hour to compensate her for her knowledge and experience."

Most operators also pay route drivers commissions as part of their regular compensation packages. "We pay above industry standard, and all our route drivers are on commission," says B.J. S.

Bonuses and Bennies

Bonuses are another popular way to both compensate and encourage. "We show employees how to make more money through proper servicing, maintaining equipment, etc.," says Wayne D. "Then we pay cash bonuses based on various factors such as limited stale quantities and proper ratio of products."

What's less common in vending are typical corporate-world benefits. "When we first started hiring employees, we had no benefits except vacation—no medical and no sick pay," Becky P. admits. "We gave one week [of vacation] for a year of service, two weeks for two years, and on up. As we grew, we added three days of sick pay. Recently, we were able to add medical insurance—we pay the employees' premiums, and they pay their dependents' premiums. I'll be perfectly honest: It's a big nut for us to cut, but with 4 percent unemployment, we had to. We couldn't get anyone of consequence without giving medical."

Fun Fact

According to a National Automatic Merchandising Association survey of member companies, hourly nonunion route driver wages ranged from $5.44 to $15.11 and averaged $9.17. Union wages ranged from $7.41 to $14.73 and averaged $11.36.

But this doesn't mean Becky left her employees without a safety net. "We have a wonderful urgent care center. When we did not have medical, [our employees went there] if they had sore throats or the flu, and we always paid it. They also have a pharmacy there, and I bought their prescriptions—the whole nine yards. I just had it set up with the doctor that he could send me the bill. In the long run, it was so infrequent, it cost a lot less than what medical insurance would have cost us."

Evaluating Performance

Regardless of what type of perks they offer, successful operators recommend basing them on concrete documentation. A written employee policy manual is a must for laying out expectations, as are proper accounting practices for tracking monetary rewards. Because writing a policy manual probably isn't your forte, obtain NAMA's complete employee guide, *Employee Policy Manual*.

As an adjunct to your employee manual, evaluate route people using a form similar to NAMA's "Self-Inspection Checklist for Machines and Location," which can be found on page 126.

B.J. S. also recommends using employee vacations to your advantage. "After 90 days with the company, route drivers are eligible for one week of vacation. I try to get them to take one week every trimester because I like to have their supervisor run the route. That way, if a driver's cheating, we find out. Unfortunately, about twice a year I let at least one person go."

To the Hard Worker Go the Spoils

With margins so tight and benefits minimal, most vending operators turn to creative ways to reward a job well done. Dinners at fancy establishments, tickets to sporting events, and company picnics complete with drawings and prizes are common choices.

In addition to such standard offerings, Becky P., the Northridge, California, operator, subsidizes new employees' Thanksgiving dinners and purchases them outright for longtime staffers. "At Easter time, they get a $25 gift certificate to the market, and I always send lilies home for their wives or—if they're young guys—for their moms.

"We try to do things centered around the family because it makes them a hero," she continues. "It's important for an employee to have the backing of his family. That way, the wife helps push him out of bed in the morning. Or when he has to work on Saturdays, the family supports him and makes arrangements to do things when he comes home.

"It gives you a better employee," Becky says. "His attitude is different toward the company. For what you get in return for what you're giving— it's tenfold."

Oh, My Aching Back

In any labor-intensive industry, injuries will happen. In bygone days, wounded workers were discarded like old rags and thus, workers' compensation insurance was born.

While most operators admit to carrying insurance for themselves, mention workers' comp and the teeth-gnashing begins. But as industry associations and publications note, employers share the blame for high workers' comp premiums.

For years, vending industry premiums soared in part because employers failed to teach and enforce basic safety practices, according to *Automatic Merchandiser*. More recently, overall safety has improved because operators began to realize the impact of "experience modification" discounts. In addition, employers are learning the value of including employees in the process of making and enforcing safety policies. After all, reductions in comp claims mean more profits and, in turn, more profit-sharing.

Workers' comp premiums are based on annual payroll and vary by state. Figure about $750 per year for a single employee who makes $10 per hour. To bring this amount down, use NAMA's publication *Developing a Work Place Safety Program* as a basis for mapping out your own safety practices. As part of your program, consider including NAMA's video *Be a Buddy to Your Back*.

Inspiring Efficiency

Motivating employees is one of the most difficult management tasks for nearly every employer. Loyalty—on the part of both employer and employee—once was the glue that bound bosses and workers. But the downsizing trend of the 1990s broke that bond, causing today's workers to be wary of long-term promises.

For employers, this means taking out the carrot and deep-sixing the stick. "We try to get [our work environment] to be a 'family' atmosphere," says B.J. S., whose employee morale was low and turnover high when he purchased the company. "Everybody knows why I'm here, why I'm doing the job the way I am, and what the goals are for the company. And they know there's room to move up and make more money."

Originally from Sweden, B.J.'s approach is born out of his European experience. "Where I grew up, the government's the safety net. But here, this [company] is the safety net. If an employee gets in trouble or needs some money, I will support them. They know they will get rewarded for their work and the company is here to protect them. For example,

Dollar Stretcher

By joining the National Automatic Merchandising Association, you'll receive discounts on a wide range of materials that will help you hire, train, and manage employees like a pro.

I have lent employees money up to $5,000, and the payment plan depends on the individual," B.J. continues. "And if someone gets hurt or has problems at home, I give them a week off with pay to straighten things out."

His reward for what others might see as a pricey system? "I haven't had any workers' comp claims since I bought the company," says B.J., the five-year owner of a decades-old operation. "And retention is better. You expect 25 percent turnover, but there was nearly 100 percent turnover when I [bought the company]."

Toughing Out Turnover

As B.J.'s comments point out, no matter how exceptional your work environment is, turnover is a fact of life. Vending wages simply can't compete with companies in hyper-growth industries like technology, and the work is demanding.

"Turnover is a big issue in today's market," Wayne D. notes. "You've always got that core of people who are going to be at work everyday," he assures. "Then there are some positions that will turn over more often—like the guy who's only been with you six months to two years."

Although every employer hits staffing slick spots, successful operators recount tale after tale of how their employees become not only valuable workers but also partners and friends.

Now that you're a hiring pro, let's explore the subject of where to locate your machines.

Self-Inspection Checklist
for Machines and Location

Company name _____

Location name _____

Adddress _____

Date of inspection _____ Route person & No. _____

Instructions: Self-inspections of locations assure your clients they are being provided with the best possible service. This checklist provides you an opportunity to show your route persons their strengths and weaknesses. It will also help you in reviewing the condition of your location and machines by pointing out a variety of items that need routine attention.

CONDITION OF LOCATION	OK	NOT OK	REMARKS
General Conditions			
Floors, platforms cleanable?	❏	❏	_____
Floors, platforms clean?	❏	❏	_____
Insects, rodents under control?	❏	❏	_____
Light adequate for servicing?	❏	❏	_____
Light adequate for customer use?	❏	❏	_____
Service Utensils & Equipment			
Cups, bowls inverted?	❏	❏	_____
Spoons wrapped or in dispenser?	❏	❏	_____
Microwave ovens clean?	❏	❏	_____
Condiments (if offered)			
Clean dispensers or packeted?	❏	❏	_____
Protected from flies, dirt?	❏	❏	_____
Trash Containers			
Adequate containers present?	❏	❏	_____
Lids, covers self-closing?	❏	❏	_____
Emptied and cleaned routinely	❏	❏	_____
Water Supply			
Approved source, safe quality?	❏	❏	_____
Connections, fittings properly installed?	❏	❏	_____

Self-Inspection Checklist
for Machines and Location, continued

CONDITION OF VEHICLE	OK	NOT OK	REMARKS
Truck compartment clean?	❑	❑	_____
Products protected?	❑	❑	_____
Perishable foods stored below 45°F?	❑	❑	_____
CO_2 tanks blocked?	❑	❑	_____
Vehicle saftey check conducted?	❑	❑	_____

EMPLOYEE CLEANLINESS

	OK	NOT OK	REMARKS
General appearance?	❑	❑	_____
Uniform clean?	❑	❑	_____
Hands clean?	❑	❑	_____
No smoking during service?	❑	❑	_____
Hands washed when necessary before servicing?	❑	❑	_____

Types of machines:

Suggested Code:

1._____ A   OK

2._____ X   Not Satisfactory

3._____ C   Corrected at Inspection

4._____ N   Does Not Apply

CONDITION OF MACHINES	MACHINE					REMARKS
	1	2	3	4	5	
Cabinet Outside						
Front, sides, top clean?	❑	❑	❑	❑	❑	_____
Delivery door, good repair?	❑	❑	❑	❑	❑	_____
Utility, bolt holes closed?	❑	❑	❑	❑	❑	_____
Vent openings screened?	❑	❑	❑	❑	❑	_____
Cabinet Inside						
Splash, spillage removed?	❑	❑	❑	❑	❑	_____
Waste pail emptied, cleaned?	❑	❑	❑	❑	❑	_____
No insects, rodents present?	❑	❑	❑	❑	❑	_____
No product left in machine?	❑	❑	❑	❑	❑	_____
Filters, cartridges, screens cleaned or exchanged routinely?	❑	❑	❑	❑	❑	_____

▲

Self-Inspection Checklist
for Machines and Location, continued

Product Containers & Piping	1	2	3	4	5	
Product surfaces, in good repair and cleanable?	❏	❏	❏	❏	❏	_____
Canisters, reservoirs, tanks, troughs, bowls, chutes, tubes, brewers, valves, pipes, etc., clean?	❏	❏	❏	❏	❏	_____
Vend stage routinely cleaned?	❏	❏	❏	❏	❏	_____

Routine Cleaning

Sanitation kit present?	❏	❏	❏	❏	❏	_____
Sanitation kit used?	❏	❏	❏	❏	❏	_____
Product contact surfaces routinely cleaned?	❏	❏	❏	❏	❏	_____
Fixed pipes, tubes, brewers properly & routinely cleaned?	❏	❏	❏	❏	❏	_____

Temperature Controls

Cold foods kept below 45° F?	❏	❏	❏	❏	❏	_____
Thermometer in cold food compartment?	❏	❏	❏	❏	❏	_____
Cut-off control operable?	❏	❏	❏	❏	❏	_____
Temperature of hot water checked periodically?	❏	❏	❏	❏	❏	_____
Ice production checked?	❏	❏	❏	❏	❏	_____

COMMODITY FILLING

Commodities correctly handled?	❏	❏	❏	❏	❏	_____
Cups properly handled, stored?	❏	❏	❏	❏	❏	_____
Food contact surfaces not touched in reloading or exchange?	❏	❏	❏	❏	❏	_____
No commodities left in machines?	❏	❏	❏	❏	❏	_____

Signature of route person at time of review_____

Date reviewed with route person_____

Supervisor conducting inspection & interview_____

Location name_____

Source: National Automatic Merchandising Association

11

Location, Location, Location

Perhaps you know the old saying about the three most important rules for purchasing property. While you're most likely to hear this adage applied to real estate, it's a mantra all successful operators keep in mind.

As we've said before, vendors are simply miniature retail stores. Given two machines of equal quality, offering the same products and serviced with the same care, the difference between one that's unprofitable and one that's profitable is where the machines are located.

John Ochi of Vernon Hills, Illinois-based Five Star Distributors puts it best: "You should be careful not to get volume just to get volume. A lot of [operators] just grab [an available location] and don't worry about it. Those are the [people] who call us up and say, 'We're going to be late making payment.'"

This isn't to say some locations are inherently bad and others good, but that a variety of factors affect whether a particular location is right for you.

Beyond Counting Heads

The size of the population at a given location once was the measuring stick for most vending specialties. With food operations, any location with more than 100 employees generally assured sufficient sales to warrant placing machines. For telecards, interstate truck stops were the prime target. However, as more operators enter any given specialty, fewer large locations remain untapped.

Today, successful operators concentrate on the quality of the population at a given location. "For example, banks have a lot of employees but they [usually] don't buy from machines," Burnsville, Minnesota, full-line operator Wayne D. explains.

As a rule of thumb, the food industry now concurs on the benchmark of 50 employees as a minimum. "There are plenty of 50-person accounts that can be profitable," assures Vince Gumma of Chicago's American Vending Sales.

In other specialties, such as telecards, your own operational costs and income goals are your best guide. "Most of my locations gross $2,000 per month in the summertime," says Preston, Washington, telecard operator Pat W. "I have very few that do less than $1,500 per month. But I know people who have locations that do $700 per month, and they're satisfied."

Does this mean completely ruling out smaller or less active locations? Not necessarily. As we've mentioned before, vending is a relationship-oriented business largely dependent on referrals as a source of new clients. Serving an underperforming location that's keen for vendors can pay off in the long run. "I have one person who owns more than one [convenience] store," illustrates Pat W. "I have a machine in one of his stores that isn't doing very well, but the client likes me, so he puts me in other stores. I could make more money

> **Tip...**
>
> **Smart Tip**
> Get information about a prospect before you even step in the door. Go to your public library or, if one's available, a dedicated business library. Seek assistance from a reference librarian, and soon you will be surrounded by an information gold mine.

somewhere else, but I choose to make that customer happy. I keep the machine in there to keep that connection."

This doesn't mean running a machine in the red. In the convenience store case, the solution was the right equipment. "Because that machine was used [when I bought it], it's not particularly attractive," Pat says. "And it's a workhorse, so it doesn't cost me much."

Since your clients are also in business and understand solvency concerns, Wayne D. suggests asking them to bring underachievers up to break-even. "If there are 20 people at the location, you tell them, 'It has to do X number of dollars, or you'll have to subsidize it.' We don't tell people they can't have a machine; we tell them it has to pay for itself, or they'll have to help pay for it."

Space in Between

Although vending operators rarely state finances in terms of hourly rates, they do stress travel time as the number one consideration when placing vendors. "I highly recommend people who are starting out don't travel outside a limited geographical area," says Wayne D. "Too many people get involved with saying, 'It's just my time, and my time isn't worth anything.' Sure your time is worth something!"

Not only does the amount of time you spend traveling define the number of machines you can service under ideal conditions, but you must also factor in trouble calls. "If you're 20 miles away, and you have to run back to fix a coin or dollar bill jam, that's an expensive proposition," says Wayne.

Telecard operator Pat W. concurs. "My furthest machine is 90 miles away. But to start out, stay close, right in your own little area. Go to the guy down the block where you're always stopping in," she advises. "Offer him a better card with a better commission. More often than you would think, people like to help people out."

Operators and experts recommend securing a sizable account and building around it. "The hub-and-spoke theory works," says Five Star Distributors' Ochi. "If you get an anchor account, you should build the spokes around it."

Who's in the Neighborhood?

Next, consider what you're up against. In food vending, this means fast-food restaurants and convenience stores. "If people in an office building can walk out and buy something in two minutes, I'll sell less," says Wayne D. "If there are 30 people on the day shift, 20 on second shift, and 25 on third shift, the third shift will buy more than the other two combined because the convenience stores aren't accessible."

Another factor is the type and amount of break time. Are employees allowed to leave the premises? Do they have an hour or a half-hour? If breaks are generous, further investigation may be in order.

Surveying the population may turn up a need for quick eats options. In a recent nationwide survey by the National Restaurant Association, nearly 40 percent of adult workers reported they did not take a real lunch break, notes the National Automatic Merchandising Association's Hudson report.

For nonfood vending, other competitive pressures warrant consideration. Baltimore pantyhose vending pioneer Janice M. says her machines compete with virtually every other purchasing option. "My market is mostly last-minute customers but not always. If I sell a good product at a good price, I get repeat customers who, instead of going to a store and buying ten pairs of hose and keeping them in their desk, might just say, 'I'll get them from the machine.' "

Purchasing Patterns

Demographics also play a starring role in locating your vendors. Since you can't carry every product known to humankind, the demographics of prospective locations speak volumes about whether or not your offerings are a good match. Gender, ethnicity, work classification, and transience are leading indicators of not only what your customers will buy but also whether they'll purchase it from a machine. "White-collar workers are more likely to go somewhere else than blue-collar," B.J. S. asserts. "It's an attitude about machine food."

To which 20-year operator Wayne D. adds, "At a high-salaried, blue-collar location—a machine shop, let's say—they will buy three times per capita [of what employees at a bank would spend]."

For telecard vendors like Pat W., who offer cards with more attractive rates than regular long-distance or wireless providers, proximity of ethnic populations is key—the more recently relocated and transient the better. "A superb location is an agricultural area where they bring pickers in to harvest crops."

> **Tip...**
>
> ## Smart Tip
>
> For information on factors that affect purchasing patterns, consult the industry organization for the products you offer. Since vending is a form of retailing, general buying trends speak volumes. And if your specialty's food, call the National Automatic Merchandising Association, (312) 346-0370, for its exhaustive report, *The Future of the Vending and Foodservice Industry 1998–2013.*

Visibility and Signage Count

For some vending specialties, another profitability factor is visibility. "To optimize sales, you want your [telecard] machines to be in plain sight," emphasizes Pat W., who primarily targets convenience stores. "You want them near the door or the counter so people inside see them and people outside can see them immediately upon entering."

Another excellent spot is next to a store's ATM, Pat says. "People have cash in their hands, and then they take one step to the right and put their money into my machine. It's a little customer service area."

Signage space is also essential. "State law and International Telecard Association guidelines say you have to have posters up," says Pat. "And merchants often request sandwich boards, banners, handouts, and oversized posters to advertise to the public."

Such materials, which card issuers often provide free of charge, explain rates and surcharges for phoning various locales. "If I carry two different cards, I make sure both posters stay up all the time," says Pat. "I tell my clients that they have to have the poster up, and they're grateful because it's hard for them to keep up with all the changes in all the laws all the time."

As you consider a location, look at its layout and determine whether there's an appropriate space for your machine and its signage. If not, it may be wise to seek greener pastures.

On the Right Route

When fuel was cheap, cities were compact, traffic was light, and the vending industry was growing, operators didn't worry much about how they organized their routes. For most operators today, all that's changed.

As the cost of travel rose, competition drove prices and margins down. Now the name of the game is reducing dead time. "We've done time studies," Wayne D. asserts. "We know it takes just as long for a guy to fill a machine with $50 of product as $100. [The significant cost] is the time getting there and opening the machine."

To bring these costs under control, the buzz is proper route structuring. Simply put, your route structure is how all your locations fit together—how often and in what order you service each location. But to be effective, you must determine the most efficient service schedule at the machine level.

"If I go to a snack machine every week for $60 dollars, the maximum I'm going to make is $3,000 annually," says Wayne D. But if that same machine is serviced every two weeks, you'll still make $60 per week and you'll have time to service a similar machine at another location, effectively doubling your sales volume. "If I go there 26 times a year [instead of 52], I'll have 26 fewer servings, 26 fewer times I count bags, and 26 fewer entries in the computer," says Wayne D. "It takes only a little

Smart Tip

No matter what you vend, always seek out ways to maximize your servicing time. "I do one location this week and one another week and two another week," says Baltimore operator Janice M. "That way I'm not stressing myself out trying to run around to six or seven different locations in one day."

more time to fill 250 items than it does 80 items. It's the time getting there—driving to the location, loading product onto a dolly, and walking into the building. If an operator doesn't learn this in the beginning he'll stumble around and never be able to properly train those he hires."

While it's logical to conclude it would be even more cost-effective to service machines once every three weeks, the cost of lost sales due to empty columns outweighs savings from fewer servicings. Generally, industry experts and trade publications suggest planning servicings for when a machine is between 50 and 60 percent of capacity.

As you may have guessed, proper route structuring doesn't necessarily mean you'll skip a location entirely. "At some locations you may fill certain machines every week and others biweekly," says Donald Blotner of Eagan, Minnesota-based DCB Consulting. "Even so, the upfront time you save on the biweekly machines can add significantly to the number of locations you're able to take on overall."

Although fine-tuning route structures is an ongoing process, the importance of considering how a prospective new location fits into current route structures can't be overstated. Of course, you can't know the exact rate or volume of sales until you actually begin servicing that location. What's important is estimating as closely as possible to determine if it's worth pursuing at all.

"It's time, time, time—in pennies, nickels, and dimes," Wayne D. stresses. "[A location] has to be right for your business."

Ochi adds, "If you aren't efficient with your route structure, you won't survive."

Steering Clear of Crime

As we discussed in Chapter 8, wear and tear on your machines affects your bottom line. A workhorse candy and snack machine can rack up sales for 20 years if it's maintained correctly and doesn't fall prey to abuse by customers or passersby.

For this reason, successful operators advise entrepreneurs to leave public locations to large operations that can better absorb the costs of insuring, repairing, and replacing easy targets. "I've seriously considered shopping malls," says Pat W. "I've had requests. Even though it meant more money, I'm so small I can't afford the risks. So I leave those to the big boys with the expensive cards."

Despite the potential for pantyhose sales, Janice M. eschews nightclubs because of the risks. "I do buildings that are very well secured, very well lit, and generally have guards."

Although you'll be stashing the cash from your vendors in a safe, being a moving target is another security concern. To compensate, Pat W. recommends choosing locations that will allow irregular servicing times. "For security reasons, I never keep a regular pickup," Pat explains. "They do not know when I'll be there."

However, Pat stresses the need to work out these arrangements in advance. Some of her clients prefer to be available when she's servicing her machines, particularly on the days she distributes commissions. In these cases Pat establishes as wide a range of options as possible. If she can't make schedules jibe, she's always found a compromise in a trusted employee who can act on the client's behalf. "But most of the time I'm able to alter my schedule to be at stores that have time parameters. Being small like this, you can do that."

Another tactic is to join your local vending association to tap into warnings about crime sprees. "We have a hotline," says John Ochi, referring to the Illinois chapter of the National Automatic Merchandising Association (NAMA). "Every time someone gets hit, the information gets distributed and at least you're forewarned. The best thing you can do is join NAMA. Even your biggest competitors will help you along because it doesn't do any of us any good in this industry when crimes happen."

What's My Cut?

Utter the word "commission" in vending circles and you'll elicit a cascade of four-letter expletives. Be that as it may, vending operators have offered clients commissions as an incentive for decades, which means clients today just plain expect to take a cut.

No matter what you're vending, commissions take as much as a 25 percent bite out of gross sales. As we discussed in Chapter 9, the average commission varies by vending specialty and geographical region as well as the size and type of client. Therefore, when you are evaluating a location, be certain to discuss your prospect's expectations upfront. Otherwise, your location may pocket your profits and leave you running in the red.

Get It in Writing

Those who look out for operators' best interests urge newbies to consider only locations willing to sign contracts. A good contract is much more than just protection from breaches of faith, such as allowing a competitor to place their machines at the same location. Instead, think of contracts as multipurpose documents. Contracts set down who is responsible for providing power so your bill acceptor works. They state commission amounts and dates when you will pay them. They lay out responsibility for damage to your

> **Bright Idea**
> If the industry organization for your specialty doesn't offer a sample contract, the makers of the popular small-business accounting software, QuickBooks, offer a solution. The Quicken Family Lawyer contains a basic business contract template and will walk you through the process of creating a document that's legal in your state.

equipment. They require your client to give you written notice of termination in advance, rather than suddenly telling you to remove your machines as you walk in for a regular servicing. And they protect your bottom line by stating your right to remove a machine if the location's unprofitable.

A written agreement also protects you from someone else's business mistakes, as Pat W. discovered the hard way. Although she originally sealed deals with a handshake, when one of her merchants went bankrupt, she switched to getting it in writing. "In order to retrieve your machine [from a property repossessed by a lender], you must prove to [the bank's attorneys'] satisfaction that you own the machine," she stresses. "Attorneys love paper. Your invoices, machine records, phone card invoices, keys, etc., are *not* enough for them. A contract is."

In short, a good contract can be used as an outline to ensure you have touched all the bases on your way from point A to point D. For an example of a detailed vending-specific contract, see NAMA's "A Guide to Location Contracts or Service Agreements" at right. A shorter format can be found on page 142, "Agreement for Sale/Lease of Goods."

Putting It All Together

Judging prospective locations can be tricky. Use the measures we've discussed here in tandem with the market research you conducted as part of Chapter 4. In addition, survey a prospect's employees, consult local demographic information, and review sales data generated by a previous vendor.

Develop an evaluation worksheet such as the "Location Evaluation" form on page 143 to help you with qualitative and quantitative analysis. When the information is all in, take a step back to see how each location fits into your business as a whole.

Remember, the more thoroughly you evaluate upfront, the more likely you are to sort the gems from the gravel. In the end, you'll be a more successful entrepreneur.

A Guide to Location Contracts or Service Agreements

In consideration of the mutual promises set out herein between the Ace Computer Company of 123 Main Street, St. Louis, Missouri, its successors and assigns, hereafter called "Location," and the ABC Vending Company of 456 Main Street, St. Louis, Missouri, its successors and assigns, hereafter called "Operator," it is agreed that:

Location grants Operator the exclusive right to sell all food, beverages, and other products and to operate a general vending service at Location's establishment at 123 Main Street, St. Louis, Missouri (hereafter called "Premises"). The Operator shall, without cost to the Location, install a sufficient number of vending machines and shall keep the machines supplied so as to adequately provide, under normal conditions, Location's employees and visitors with sufficient amounts of food, beverages, and other products of good quality, prepared and dispensed in compliance with all local, state, and federal health and sanitation standards. Operator shall provide through its vending machines merchandise that is reasonably priced and offered in reasonably sized portions.

Utilities, Equipment, and Furniture

Location shall, at its own expense, provide Operator all necessary utility outlets in the areas where equipment is to be located and shall also furnish without cost to Operator all necessary heat, hot and cold water, gas, lights, and electric current and will permit interruption in such services only in cases of emergency. Location agrees to notify Operator immediately of any interruption or proposed interruption of such services.

Operator shall have the right at any reasonable time to remove, replace, or add, as Operator deems necessary, to the vending machines and other equipment installed under this agreement. Operator shall notify Location of such change. Vending machines and other equipment installed by Operator under this agreement and their contents are and shall remain the property of Operator.

Operator shall purchase and install chairs, tables, and other stands and auxiliary equipment for furnishing food-service areas at the premises. The number, cost, and design of such furniture shall be approved by Location prior to purchase. Operator shall furnish Location with evidence of payment in full for the furniture. Operator shall be reimbursed for the cost of the furniture by the retention of _____ % of the monthly payments payable to Location until such time as the cost plus _____ % of the interest on the unpaid balance is repaid. Location shall have the right at any time to make addition payments to repay the cost. If this agreement is terminated for any reason prior to complete reimbursement to Operator, the unpaid balance will become due and payable 30 days after termination. Title shall remain in Operator until complete reimbursement has been made.

Continued on next page

Compensation, Accounting, Licenses, Cost Changes

Operator agrees to pay Location the following sums subject to other provisions of this agreement:

_____% of gross receipts or

_____% of gross receipts of (Product)

(list each Product)

The term "gross receipts" shall not include any applicable sales or use taxes.

Operator will report on the basis of 13 four-week accounting periods, and will submit within 20 days after the close of each such period to Location a report of gross receipts through the machines together with a check for the sum due Location under this agreement. Operator shall maintain an accurate record of all merchandise, inventories, and receipts in connection with performance under this agreement. Location is authorized to inspect such records at all reasonable times during business hours.

Operator agrees to obtain and display, if required, all applicable federal, state, and local licenses.

It is understood that compensation paid to Location under this agreement is based on federal, state, and local taxes and license fees and on the cost of merchandise sold through the machine existing at the date of this agreement. In the event of an increase in taxes, license fees, or the cost of merchandise sold through the machines under this agreement, which are not reflected in an increase in the retail selling price, then the compensation to Location provided for in this agreement shall be reduced to reflect such increases.

Maintenance and Sanitation

Operator shall operate and maintain all vending machines and other equipment in a clean, sanitary condition in accordance with recognized standards for such machines in accordance with all applicable laws and regulations. Location will keep the areas in which the vending machines are located in all service areas in a clean and sanitary condition and shall dispose of all refuse that results from the operation of the vending service and will replace expendable items as needed.

Personnel

Operator's personnel will at all times be dressed in clean, neat uniforms and will observe all regulations in effect on Premises. Operator shall not employ at the Premises any employee not acceptable to Location. Operator's employees shall have health examinations as frequently and as thoroughly as required by law and good practice. Location agrees to furnish Operator's personnel with any identification

Continued on next page

passes required for entrance to and exit from the Premises. Location shall not impose any regulations on Operator's personnel not imposed on Location's personnel. The parties hereto agree that they will not hire employees of the other within six months of the date of termination of their employment with the other without the written permission of the other party.

Indemnity

Operator will indemnify and hold Location, its employees, guests, and visitors harmless for any loss, damage, injury, or liability occurring because of the negligent performance by Operator's employees, contractors, or agents under this agreement. Location will pay Operator all losses from theft of money and merchandise and from vandalism or other intentional damage of Operator's vending machines and other equipment. In no case, however, shall Location's liability for such losses exceed the lower of 1) the repair or replacement cost of machines and equipment damaged plus the value of money and merchandise lost or 2) $_____ per occurrence.

Insurance

Operator will procure and maintain the following insurance:

(a) Worker's Compensation as prescribed by the laws of the State of Missouri.

(b) Comprehensive bodily injury, property damage, liability, and casualty loss, with limits of $_____ for injury or death of one person and $_____ for injury or death of two or more persons in any one accident; and $_____ property damage in any one accident.

(c) Product liability as shall protect Operator and Location, their employees, agents, and independent contractors in minimum limits of $_____.

Location shall promptly notify Operator in writing of any claims against either Location or Operator, and in the event of a suit being filed, shall promptly forward to Operator all papers in connection therewith. Location shall not incur any expense or make any settlement of any such claims or suit without Operator's consent.

Alterations

Location agrees to notify Operator of any alteration that will affect any of the areas where services are performed under this agreement before such alterations are made. Operator agrees to make no alterations in the premises unless authorized in writing by Location. Location agrees to cooperate in making any alterations that may become necessary for proper performance of the service under this agreement.

Continued on next page

▲

A Guide to Location Contracts or Service Agreements, continued

Term, Renewal, Business Interruption: Cancellation and Breach

This agreement shall become effective _____ and remain in force for a period of three years and for any additional period due to business interruption. Unless canceled by written notice at least _____ days prior to the termination date, this agreement is deemed to be automatically renewed for additional periods of one year thereafter upon the same terms as set out herein.

If, because of riots, war, public emergency or calamity, fire, earthquake, or other Acts of God, government restrictions, labor disturbances, or strikes, operations at Premises are interrupted or stopped, performance of this agreement, with the exception of money due, shall be suspended and excused for so long as such interruption or stoppage continues. This agreement shall be extended for a period of time equal to the time of the interruption or stoppage.

Either party to this agreement may terminate this agreement by giving _____ days notice in writing to the other party of its intention to cancel this agreement. This agreement may also be terminated by Operator by reason of unprofitability by giving _____ days written notice to Location.

In the event any provisions of this agreement are violated by either party, the other party shall serve written notice upon the breaching party setting forth the violation and demanding compliance with the agreement. Unless within _____ days after serving such notice, such violations cease and corrections are made, the aggrieved party may terminate this agreement immediately by written notice to the offending party.

Termination

Upon termination of this agreement, Operator shall vacate the Premises and shall return the Premises together with all furniture owned by Location to the same condition as when originally made available to Operator, normal wear and tear, fire, and other casualty loss excepted. If Operator fails to remove its property and effects within a reasonable time after termination, Location shall have the right to remove and store Operator's property and effects at the expense of Operator.

Damages

It is understood and agreed that Operator has incurred, in anticipation of sales to be made over the term of this agreement, expenses in purchasing and installing machines and other equipment, hiring or rescheduling employees, purchasing inventory, and other expenses. It is understood and agreed that these expenses form part of the consideration for this agreement. In the event this agreement is canceled, or terminated by breach by the Location prior to its termination date,

Continued on next page

A Guide to Location Contracts
or Service Agreements, continued

Operator shall be entitled, as a measure of the expenses incurred and earnings lost as agreed by the parties hereto for such period, to recover 1) any unamortized expenses for machines and other equipment installed under this agreement plus 2) _____% of the average monthly gross receipts or sales made through the machines during the months prior to such cancellation or breach to the date this agreement would have terminated had there been no cancellation or breach.

Miscellaneous

It is understood and agreed that this contract establishes an independent contractor relationship between the parties. Notices to Location required herein shall be addressed to the Ace Computer Company, 123 Main Street, St. Louis, Missouri. Notices to Operator required herein shall be addressed to the ABC Vending Company, 456 Main Street, St. Louis, Missouri.

This agreement shall be construed under the laws of the State of Missouri.

This agreement is entered into by Operator on the expressed representation that Location owns the business at the Premises or has the authority to enter into this agreement.

This agreement constitutes the entire agreement between the parties and all previous communications between the parties with respect to this agreement are cancelled and superseded.

Witness our hands this _____ day of _____, 200x.

_____	_____
Operator	Location
_____	_____
By	By
_____	_____
Address	Address
_____	_____
City, State	City, State

Source: National Automatic Merchandising Association

Agreement for Sale/Lease of Goods

Memo Form

Agreement made_____, through _____, between
                          month/day/year   month/day/year

_____ and _____
Name of Buyer   Name of Seller
herein referred to as buyer, of   herein referred to as seller, of

Address _____   Address _____

City_____   City_____

County_____   County _____

State_____   State _____

This memo confirms the sale/purchase or lease on: _____
                                                        Month/Day/Year

Quantity   List items being purchased/leased:

_____   _____

_____   _____

_____   _____

for_____ Dollars ($_____)

Is this a deposit?   ❑ Yes   ❑ No

Deposit will be returned upon removal of all vending equipment in good condition from location and if purchased deposit will be applied toward purchase.

Dated_____ month/day/year

Signature of Buyer   Signature of Seller

_____   _____

Source: McLean Machines & Co. Inc.

Location Evaluation

These are important questions for you to ask each location owner or manger. This enables you to evaluate if it would be profitable for you to pursue this account.

Company name _____

Contact _____

Address _____

Phone _____

Location_____

Employees _____ Shifts_____

Hours open_____ Weekends_____

% Male _____ % Female_____

Average age _____

Eat/drink at location? _____

Leave building? _____

How long lunch? _____

Breaks? _____ How long? _____

Nearby fast food?_____

Cafeteria? _____

Food trucks? _____

Reasons for change _____

_____

Referred by? _____

Equipment the customer requests _____

_____

Commission requested? _____

Willing to sign agreement or contract? _____

Notes: _____

_____

Evaluation by _____ Date _____

Source: The Vending Connection

Blow Your
Horn

Most businesses have only one target
audience—either the mass market they sell to anonymously or
a small group of buyers they serve one-on-one. As you already
know, vending entrepreneurs sell to both.

▲

Because of your unique dual-clientele situation, blowing your own horn means marketing to the first group and merchandising to the second group. As the industry magazine *Automatic Merchandiser* explains it, marketing is determining who you're selling your product to and how you're going to do it. Merchandising is determining the exact brand, color, flavor, size, type, and quantity someone wants to buy and then presenting it to them in a manner that encourages them to do so.

Since you must market your vendors effectively before you can merchandise the products in them, in this chapter we'll talk about marketing and leave merchandising for the following chapter.

But before we move on, it's important to note your marketing strategies should be relationship-based. Sage operators advise against using direct-mail letters, newspaper ads, or other relatively anonymous forms of mass advertising. Instead, your main approach will be cold-calling, contacting prospects directly by telephone or in person.

Build on the Basics

Before you pick up the phone to make inquiries or slip on your dress shoes to pound the pavement, invest in the marketing essentials. For any successful entrepreneur, the most basic marketing tools are also the most valuable, and in vending, this means business cards, Yellow Pages ads, and vehicle signage.

- *Business cards.* Whether you whip them up on your computer or use a print shop, business cards are the currency of the marketing trade. Handing a prospect a business card (or mailing them one to follow up a phone conversation) shows you are as serious a businessperson as they are. Without a card, you're just a wanna-be—someone who's not serious and can't be trusted to be there tomorrow.

- *Yellow Pages ads.* As a serious businessperson, you'll already have a business telephone line, which means you are automatically eligible for a Yellow Pages listing. "It's a given that your competitors will screw up," points out Donald Blotner of Eagan, Minnesota-based DCB Consulting. "There are plenty of bad vending companies out there, which is the reason why vending has such a bad reputation. Because there is always somebody looking for a new vendor, you better be in the book."

- *Vehicle signage.* The more time commuters spend in their cars, the more valuable your vehicle's exterior becomes. Let's face it—you want the beleaguered procurement officer who's unhappy with his current vending operator to spot your sportster and write down your telephone number. "Most companies of any worth will feel proud to put their names on the trucks," comments Burnsville, Minnesota, full-line operator Wayne D. "Also, many people don't want you running in and out of their buildings unless they know who you are."

All set? Good. Now it's time to ponder your next moves.

Who Do You Know?

Consensus within our group of operators and experts mirrors marketing wisdom for any industry: Your initial efforts should target those you know. Not only is this tactic more likely to net you paying accounts, but you'll also hone your presentation skills on individuals most likely to cut you some slack.

As equipment distributor Vince Gumma of Chicago's American Vending Sales puts it, "Usually, when new operators come in to [purchase equipment from] us, they have something already lined up—a friend or relative at a factory or office building—and they've got some kind of verbal commitment." In fact, waiting until you've made your first sale makes good business sense. After all, Gumma points out, you won't know the right machines to purchase until you've evaluated the location.

Baltimore pantyhose vending innovator Janice M. turned to her own congregation. "My first [client] was my church. They were willing to give me a shot, and I was so happy. I still have that same account."

Wayne D. tapped into contacts he was making as a sales representative for R.J. Reynolds. "Once we established the business, there was a lot of word-of-mouth—people began to refer us to other people." The experience of these operators clearly supports the importance of drawing on your existing relationships.

Targeting Prospects

After you have pitched your services to those you know, you are ready for total strangers. Use your market research from Chapter 4 to generate prospects.

"I basically go after large buildings with a lot of women who circulate throughout the building," says pantyhose operator Janice M. of her prospecting tactics. "Every week, the *Baltimore Business Journal* compiles lists such as 'the biggest warehouses,' 'the biggest female-owned workplaces,' or 'the biggest churches.' They break the lists down into categories so you can see the number of female employees, total employees, where they're located, and what they do. That generally tells me a little bit about the company and helps me make a decision."

Some operators turn to locators, individuals who do the sleuthing work for a fee. "We use a telemarketer who's a friend of ours," explains Northridge, California, full-line operator Becky P. "We pay his telephone bill and 10 percent of the first month's gross at each location he generates for us."

However, as trade magazine *Automatic Merchandiser* points out, unless you've thoroughly evaluated a locator's reputation, beware. Blue Sky

Smart Tip

Even if your very first sales call will be on your favorite uncle, practice your presentation out loud before your meeting. Actually speaking the words ferrets out tongue-twisters, inspires confidence, and smoothes out your delivery.

outfits often found in the "Business Opportunities" newspaper classifieds have charged tens of thousands of dollars to place vendors in locations where they do nothing but rust, sending not a few unsuspecting newbies into bankruptcy.

While a locator, such as Becky's, who takes a cut of actual sales is more likely to be reputable than one who demands money upfront, the only way to be sure is to seek out industry advice. Reputable locators are becoming more common, and some start-ups have grown into handsome enterprises with the assistance they've received. If you're interested in getting help from a locator, contact the National Automatic Merchandising Association for guidance.

> ### Bright Idea
>
> Before your first sales call, recruit a friend, older child, spouse, or anyone who can keep a straight face, to role-play the part of a prospective client. The more skepticism your guinea pig can muster, the more thoroughly you'll be prepared for the real thing!

Making the Calls

Armed with as much advance information about your prospects as you can dig up, now it's time to start cold-calling.

"You call the customer and find out if the contact person [for vending] is the one who's listed [from your research]; most likely it's not," says Hendersonville, Tennessee, full-line operator B.J. S. After you determine who the correct contact is, you ask to speak to them. "You tell them who you are and ask them if you can send information. You find out pretty quick if they're interested or not," B.J. continues. "They'll tell you, no, I'm under contract or I'm happy with the service I have."

Although phone calls save time and, often, gasoline, some newbies to the cold-calling process prefer to start off with a more personal approach.

"The first thing you ask is who's the contact regarding your vending needs—it may be the owner of the company; it may be the secretary; it may be the facilities manager. It may be an apartment manager. It depends on where you're going," Wayne D. asserts.

"If possible, survey the location. Do they have old equipment there? What can you offer that the current operator doesn't offer?" continues the full-line operator from the Twin Cities. "Then, just walk in, drop your business card off and say, 'If you're dissatisfied with your current vendor, give me a call. I'd like to make a proposal to you. If you are satisfied, maybe I can satisfy you better.'"

For a sample calling script, see page 149.

Rhino Hide

As the scenarios presented by our operators suggest, cold-callers quickly develop thick skins. Successful salespeople also take rejection in stride.

Calling Script

Now That We've Got Your Attention!

Did you know that vending machines are a $25 billion business per year?

And in this case the best business offer you'll ever get! Here's why:

A-1 Vending Machines is a new and innovative company whose marketing concept is new to the market and very much in demand and growing larger everyday.

If you would like to be a pioneer in change, then I would like to welcome you to A-1 Vending Machines. We are a company that markets pantyhose through vending machines.

Benefit to you? Quality of product! Service and convenience to employees!

Benefit to you is that our machine will offer the opportunity to make money;

Do a great job 24 hours a day;

Will work 24 hours a day seven days a week 365 days a year;

Will not ask for a pay raise;

Tell you how to run your business;

Have a bad day; or

Sleep, eat, take vacations, or be late to work.

In fact our pantyhose machines will even cut down on instances of that for most of your female employees.

Example: Instead of stopping off at a local store or taking a break during work hours or long lunch, employees can get pantyhose from our machines located in the restroom of your establishment out of plain view.

Our machines also offer a very highly recommended brand of nylons.

We offer many different selections at a variable, competitive price.

We aim to make the buyer and his consumers happy, which is why as a good customer relations base, we include surveys in all our products during the first three months to make sure our service is the best.

Continued on next page

Calling Script, continued

Your employees will love you and look at your company in more personable favor because they then know, or at least think, you care about them enough to make everyday life easier for them, which increases your productivity among employees for several reasons:

1. Frees more time to work

2. Enables as professional a look as possible

3. Says to outside consumers and business prospects you care about your employees

What is in it for you?

- ○ Opportunity to make good profit on a constant basis

- ○ Opportunity to generate substantial dollars that can be channeled into many different morale boosting activities, such as parties, employee fund-raisers, picnics, or any special functions that your office or company may be trying to raise money for

- ○ Opportunity to generate funds on a daily basis and also plug into the largest cash business in the world!

As mentioned previously, vending is a $25 billion a year business. By general standards, this guarantees you to make some amount of profit even if you do not hit $25 billion.

How hard will you work? Your job will consist of opening up the cash slot, retrieving your money, and locking the machine back up.

A-1 Vending Machines will handle restocking the machine and maintenance.

Also keep in mind our machines are not meant to replace your current business, unless that is your choice, but rather as additional revenue raisers for whatever the reason.

Source: McLean Machines & Co. Inc.

Over the five years since he purchased the business from his father-in-law, B.J. S. collected statistics on his sales calls. "I keep track of every sales call on my computer—what I did, what I talked about. You get somebody interested every 40 phone calls, so that's the success rate—one in 40. You have to have some type of sense of humor," he continues. "Part of sales is being persistent and never giving up. Some of these guys know I'm going to call them every four months. You have to be stubborn as hell and not take 'No' for an answer."

Telecard operator Pat W., of Preston, Washington, receives the most resistance from merchants who are already selling cards at the counter. "They don't believe they'll do better with a 20 percent commission on machine sales instead of 25 percent over the counter." Because she knows the immediacy of the machine is more attractive to consumers than waiting in line to purchase a telecard at the counter, Pat doesn't let the over-the-counter (OTC) argument deter her. "A vendor always outsells OTC," she remarks.

To illustrate, Pat recounts the tale of an OTC merchant who declined a vendor because he sold fewer than a dozen cards a month. "I said, 'If you suspend OTC sales for six weeks, I'll put in a machine and we'll see what happens.' In the first month, the location sold 50 cards from a two-column machine. Now they have a four-column, and when I go in the store, the merchant smiles."

Promoting a Concept

For those pioneering new vending frontiers, changing a no to a yes can hinge on your ability to show your prospects a benefit they might not immediately see. Pat W. discovered one hook was promising increased customer traffic. "I'd tell [convenience store] merchants [telecard buyers] are going to come back for more cards and then they'll buy a few more things."

With pantyhose vending, presenting the concept as an employee benefit is crucial. Says Janice M., "When I'm calling and the response is, 'He's not in. What are you calling for?' I say, 'My name is Janice and I offer a new service for your female employees. We sell pantyhose vending machines.' And especially if it's a female assistant, they usually go, 'Oh, pantyhose? Oh yeah, that's great!' Generally they say, 'I'll take your name and number and I will have him call you. Or if you want you can send some information in and I will make sure he looks at it.'"

Smart Tip

Tip...

Anyone who's worked in the corporate world knows the receptionists, administrative assistants, etc. are the ones who keep a company running. Often, they'll also be your vendor's best customers. Rather than trying to bypass these gatekeepers, give them your pitch—start to finish. Showing assistants a little respect makes them allies and helps net you the sale.

Bright Idea

If you purchase a color multifunction machine (printer/fax/copier/scanner) as recommended in Chapter 7, producing a colorful proposal is no longer cost-prohibitive. Applying a splash of color to your logo, proposal headings, clip art, or simple charts and graphs is as easy as touching a key.

Post-Call to-Dos

When you hit one of those one-in-40 responses, B.J. S. recommends being ready to go into high gear. "Obviously, when someone says, 'Send me information,' you have to have something nice to send them. Instead of just sending them a flier, you have to make up a nice proposal that's multicolored."

Incorporate as much information as possible about how your prospect will benefit from your service and supply a list of trade references—clients, your banker, suppliers, a relative who's a business owner, or anyone you have established a solid relationship with.

"Include everything except machine information because you haven't seen their break room yet, and you don't really know their needs," advises B.J. But do furnish a listing of machines you carry (or plan to purchase) along with some narrative drawn from marketing materials supplied by the equipment manufacturer. "In that section, you say you want to meet with them to see their break room and see how you can fit the machines to their needs." Write a cover letter and place it on top of the proposal.

Janice M. expands on this advice. "I include a general introduction, pros and cons of having a pantyhose vending machine, why we think it works, and articles that have been written about me as well as customers and their comments." What she doesn't mention in her proposals is the availability of commissions. "Some clients want commissions and others don't. I try to figure out the person I'm meeting with and go from there."

If you're answering an RFP (request for proposal), the process of assembling a proposal is essentially the same. However, with an RFP you must speak to each point, even if you normally withhold such information until you meet. Failing to address a point in an RFP is a red flag to a prospect—you might as well be stating you're unconcerned with meeting their needs.

Assistance with preparing proposals and answering RFPs is available from NAMA or your specialty-specific industry association. See above for a sample cover letter to send with your proposal.

Asking for the Sale

Once you've sent a proposal, don't sit on your hands waiting for your phone to ring. The name of the game is follow-up. Prospects expect you to call.

Says Janice, "When I call back and I say, 'I sent you information; did you receive it?' they usually say, 'Yes. Can you come in and talk with us?' At that point, I pretty much know I have a sale or there's interest in it. If they don't invite you to come in, then they don't want to hear about it."

To ensure your follow-ups are timely, construct a simple system for recording your prospecting activities. A sample of such a form, "Contact Sheet for New Clients," is on page 155.

Sealing the Deal

Although one of the attractions of operating a vending business is casual attire, successful entrepreneurs emphasize preparing for your sit-downs by dressing for success.

Cover Letter

March 5, 200x

Mr. Gordon Bleu
1111 Market Street
Baltimore, MD

Dear Mr. Bleu,

Enclosed please find some information on A-1 Vending Machines, a pantyhose vending service. Let us show you how to profit from space you already own and impress your female employees at the same time.

My name is Jill Smith. I will call you when I am in your area to see if we can meet and discuss which opportunities will work for you.

Thank you in advance for your time. I look forward to talking with you soon.

Sincerely,

Jill Smith

Jill Smith

Enclosures

Source: McLean Machines & Co. Inc.

"Once I went out on a Monday to meet with a prospect and we agreed to put machines in that Thursday," recalls Wayne D. "On Thursday I put a pair of overalls on to help put in the machines. [When he saw us moving the machines in] the client said, 'Aren't you the guy who came in on Monday to talk to me about putting in the machine?' "

In addition to her verbal presentation, Janice M. provides a visual aid to help sell her breakthrough concept. "I have a videotape that shows me and the machines. And it has footage of various local TV shows I've been on. It's 16 minutes long and cost $120 to edit. Now I'm working on a more detailed one of me filling the machine, putting the money in, etc., to show the efficiency of the product, and that one's about five minutes."

Reputation Sells

As we've mentioned before, successful vending entrepreneurs guard their reputations with their lives. Even early on, veterans say a good reputation is all that matters.

"When you're starting out, your clients are going to be your best source of new business," stresses 20-year veteran Wayne D. "If you've satisfied them, they're going to recommend you because there are enough poor vending companies out there that there are always bids available. Even today, we get 60 percent of our business through referrals."

B.J. S. emphatically agrees. "The biggest selling point in vending is word-of-mouth. Having a good reputation [is key]. A lot of our business is people who have had a different vending company, and then they come to us."

Nonfood operators also agree. "I had a person ask me to take a machine out because they were going to go with cheaper cards," Pat W. recounts. "After three months, they called back and said that their customers didn't like the new cards, so would I put my machine back in. I did, and there were no hard feelings. My concern must not only be for my bottom line, but first and foremost for the end user and the merchant," she continues. "That is why I get referrals."

"I'm very blunt about it when we talk the first time," says the Seattle-area operator. "I say, 'If you don't like me, give me 30 days' notice and I'll leave. If I don't like you, I'll give you 30 days and I'll leave.' I guarantee my cards and my service and guarantee they can get out of it whenever they want. I'm told the big companies require them to lease the machine and keep it stocked, and they can't get out of it. By allowing them to give 30 days' notice, I've never had anything but goodwill in return."

A Word on Being Wired

Few vending operations, large or small, have yet to embrace the Internet. Low-tech by nature, most operators simply don't believe the Web is a useful marketing tool.

Contact Sheet for New Clients

Date	Name & Type of Company	Contact Person	Phone	Result

Source: McLean Machines & Co. Inc.

Here's where savvy entrepreneurs can gain a competitive advantage. While you may have little interest in surfing the Internet, your prospects are almost certainly wired. Many of them will already be addicted to e-mail as a form of communication.

For small-business owners, designing a Web site once required hiring a highly paid guru. Now, e-mail providers like AOL make creating a simple site as easy as point and click. Those worth their salt also throw in the tools to create a site and toll-free technical support to talk you through the process—a marketing and, as we'll discuss in a later chapter, customer service bargain at $19.95 per month.

Introducing Yourself

After you ink a contract at a new location, take a final marketing step. Broadcast your new service to the crew on location.

"We place signage on our machines saying a new vending company is here," Wayne D. says. "In a factory setting, we place signs around the building. In an office building, we pass out fliers. On all of them, we say, 'Call our office and tell us what you want.' "

Introducing yourself to your potential customers serves the same purpose as any other marketing effort: encouraging customers to buy. Blowing your own horn is especially critical in circumstances where a previous operator may not have delivered as high a level of service as you do. While you have obviously convinced the boss you're the best, the only way employees will know is if you tell them.

Hook, Line, and Sinker

Although you will develop your own techniques for sealing the deal, here's how one operator gets the job done:

"When I approach a prospect, I have my business card in my hand, my [commissions] record book under my arm, pictures of my machines, and a bundle of [defective] telecards," explains Pat W. "I go to the owner [of the store or shop], offer my hand and introduce myself, my company, and my service. I tell him we offer the best, most reliable and stable cards along with a variety of programs to help him make money. If they've already got telecards, I'll say, '*More money.*' Because they all want to make money, they listen to me," she chuckles. "So we sit down and I show him the cards that I carry. I tell him I use these particular cards because of their attractive national and international rates."

Then Pat asks the client questions. "I ask how much walk-in traffic he has each day, what his market is—truckers, day-trippers, residents of the apartments next door. And I ask about special cultural needs. Of course I know some of this already from my own

---

Good Vibrations

Public relations is a misunderstood and underutilized marketing tool. Although many people define PR as an article in the newspaper, in truth it's much more.

What doesn't work? In vending circles, special events such as grand openings, celebrity appearances, and holiday gatherings are rarely used because they require attractive commercial office space, which start-up operators usually lack. It's also generally ineffective to seek media attention. The media's job is covering the "new" or the "novel," and most vending operations are neither. (Caveat: If you're starting an operation in a smaller city, your local newspaper might want to know.)

What does work? For most operators, one key PR tactic is cause-related marketing. As the name implies, cause-related marketing is allying yourself with a worthy cause. To be effective, you must choose causes of interest to your prospects. For example, if your market is health-care clinics, supply snacks or sodas to a fundraising event for a cancer center, hospice, etc. This entitles you to attend and network. After the event, distribute a news release to doctors and clinic administrators telling precisely how your donation benefited the fundraiser.

Be sure to include a run-down of your charitable efforts in your sales proposals, as well. And remember to write off the cost of the inventory on your taxes.

Another vital strategy is one-on-one networking. "To get to know people in the community, get involved in the Optimists, Rotary, VFW, American Legion, Shriners, etc.," advocates Burnsville, Minnesota, operator Wayne D.

Joining your local chamber and shaking hands at monthly after-hours events also helps. Participating in appropriate professional association activities, such as trade shows for corporate procurement directors, is also wise.

▲

Grabbing the Spotlight

If you're serving a specific community or population in a unique way—as is Northridge, California, full-line operator Becky P., with her unique approach to nonnative speakers (more about this in Chapter 13)—or if you're pioneering a new specialty, such as Baltimore operator Janice M.'s pantyhose vending concept, the media will want to hear.

"Initially I talked to a reporter from the *Baltimore Business Journal*," explains Janice. "I ran into him at a small-business seminar, and after I started my business, I went through my business cards and gave him a call.

"He wrote a story about me, and I got a new customer from his column," she continues. "Later on, I got a call from Channel 13, our ABC-TV affiliate, which saw the story in the *Baltimore Business Journal*. Then, the *Baltimore Sun* got it from Channel 13. After that, our NBC-TV affiliate did a story, and then the NBC radio affiliate did one. Then the CBS-TV affiliate called and, finally, *Black Enterprise* magazine."

From there, word-of-mouth took off, and Janice's marketing efforts soared. Enthuses the entrepreneur, "Since then, I've done local cable access talk shows, local radio station talk shows, and interviews for the local and national black press."

research," she confides. "But I learn about him and his knowledge. Also, asking questions shows I'm listening to him and am interested in his needs.

"Then I tell him about the merits of the cards and how he'll attract more people to the store once the cards are there," Pat says. "I tell him there are several ways to make money. I can sell cards to him and he can sell them over the counter. I can supply him with the cards on consignment and he can sell them over the counter. 'Or,' I say as I pull out a picture, 'I can make it completely hassle-free by installing a vending machine.'

"At this point, he'll usually say he's had other machines and he thinks they're ugly," says Pat. "I reply that my machines are secure, they look professional, and I like to service upscale locations that are well kept, which puts him in the category of being 'upscale.' "

Next, Pat offers her prospect photos of other, less attractive machines and remarks, "I think one that looks professional and is dependable goes best with a conservative, stable, and reliable business. To which the potential client will say something like 'I like this machine' and almost invariably they'll choose the one I've recommended."

When she begins to discuss the cards themselves, her prospects often compare them to others. "They'll say, 'I've seen such and such down the street that are cheaper.' I respond with 'I'll show you a dozen that are cheaper,' and I haul out my bundle of bad cards and say, 'All of these were cheaper and they all went out of business.'" While this illustrates the adage "You get what you pay for," Pat warns that even name brands go belly-up.

"I promise to keep him [informed] on what's going on in the industry and tell him more about the industry in general," she continues. "This makes him feel very smart because he's not going with cards just because they have a big name."

A devotee of the sales trainer Zig Ziglar, Pat says his strategy works. "He says if you give people what's useful to them—if you can make them feel good, make them laugh, and make them feel smart—they'll do business with you."

Pat's anecdotal evidence supports Ziglar's claims. "Usually I don't even get through the sales pitch or tell them everything he needs to know. Putting them in the upscale crowd is enough. They just get up and say, 'Where can we put the vendor?' and start walking around the store."

Contact NAMA and specialty-specific associations, such as the International Telecard Association, for more tips and advice on your personal marketing strategy.

Smart Tip

Tip...

Whenever you make a sales pitch, provide opportunities for your prospect to talk. Ask questions, listen attentively, and take notes. This shows your client you're interested in what he or she wants, not just what you want. At the same time, the data you collect will help you determine what will be profitable and what won't.

13

Getting Them
to Buy

Whether you're reading this book cover to cover or consulting it step by step, the first thing to know about merchandising is it's the most important ingredient to your vending operation's success. You can place the nicest machines in the most lucrative locations, but if people don't buy what you're selling, you'll quickly be a has-been.

Photo© Automatic Products International Ltd.

Fortunately, when it comes to merchandising, you're not going where no one's been before. The tools and advice you'll need are readily available. Best of all, the concepts are easy to learn and apply.

Because food vendors, from snacks and soda to frozen desserts, offer more selections than other specialty machines, we're going to use edibles to explain merchandising basics. However, the techniques you employ to maximize sales in a 20-column snack machine also apply to a four-column telecard unit, except it's all less complicated with a four-column device.

Merchandising 101

As we mentioned in the previous chapter, merchandising is determining the exact brand, color, flavor, size, type, and quantity of products your customers want to buy and then presenting them to consumers in a manner that encourages them to do so.

"If we have a facility that has all truck drivers and blue-collar workers, we would not merchandise the same items in a heavily female area," says Burnsville, Minnesota, full-line operator Wayne D. "In a predominantly female location, we'd offer more low-fat items and diet sodas. In Hispanic areas, there'd be different items than Asian areas."

In addition to the right products for your customers, proper merchandising means stocking the right amount of items. "If chips are the biggest item, then I need to put more rows of chips in the machine," Wayne D. says. "If a location needs more Cheetos, we'll give you three rows of Cheetos. You may see two or three empty columns, but that's because people are buying more Cheetos."

Of course, product presentation plays a major role in merchandising. "If you put sandwiches in a machine on a Monday, and you don't show up to service the machine until Friday, no one's going to touch that machine after Tuesday," explains Northridge, California, full-line operator Becky P.

And just as grocery stores offer specials on certain items to introduce new offerings or encourage increased buying, the same goes for vended items. "It can be as simple as putting up a sign that says, 'New this month,'" suggests Donald Blotner of Eagan, Minnesota-based DCB Consulting. "Or offering 'discount day' where everything's half price."

Stocking by the Numbers

Not surprisingly, the goal of proper merchandising is selling the maximum amount of products while limiting out-of-stock columns. An empty column isn't selling anything, and if it remains empty too long, it essentially sends the message "Don't trust this machine; seek what you want elsewhere."

To know what to stock the very first time, rely on statistics compiled by your suppliers or information you've gathered as part of your market research. To illustrate, let's use the "Quality Snacks Start-Up Inventory Expenses" form on page 114 in Chapter 9, which shows a sample starting inventory for a 654-unit snack machine as proposed by Chicago's Five Star Distributors. Regional statistics gathered by Five Star show 54.1 percent of purchases will be candy/snack bars, 15.3 percent will be gum and mints, 9.2 percent pastries, 7.65 percent cookies/crackers/snacks, 7.65 percent salty snacks, and 6.1 percent large single-serving salty snacks.

Therefore, if you were an operator in the Chicago area with a 654-unit snack vendor, the first time you fill the machine you'd need 354 units of candy/snack bars, 100 units of gum and mints, 60 units of pastries, 50 units of cookies/crackers/snacks, 50 units of salty snacks, and 40 units of large single-serving salty snacks.

As you will recall from Chapter 11, it is recommended that a machine be serviced (filled)

Beware!
Empty spirals are the sworn enemy of operators. "If it's merchandised properly, there will be the right amount of chips, candy, etc., for what people are buying," stresses Burnsville, Minnesota, full-line operator Wayne D. "If not, you need to change the configurations to reduce out-of-stock."

Route Cards/Delivery Receipts

Route cards or delivery receipts, such as the samples below, are vital to tracking inventory and merchandising effectively.

RTE	SERV #	SERV TYPE	CHANGER AMT	EMPLOYEE				MACH #	MACH DESC		MACH #
3	16	COLLECT	33.00					1879	SNACK LFT		1879
DATE		WEEK	DAY	LOCATION							RTE/SERV. #
11/18/99		1	THU								3/16
PRODUCT		G&M	CHIP	CNDY	COOK	SNKS	DEBY	BAG	G&M		WEEK 1
PRICE:		0.50	0.60	0.65	0.75	0.75	0.60	1.00	0.75		DAY THU
PAR		60	99	534	15	15	30	45	20		11/18
FILLS											(CHECK ONE)
											REFUND
DAMAGED											CHARGE
REMOVED											C.O.D.
INVENTORY											
METER 1 READING				METER 2 READING			TESTS	REFUNDS		CASH COLLECTED	AMOUNT
CONTACT					SERV TIME	BEG	END	SLUGS	CASH COMM		
COMPANY NAME MIDWEST VENDING, INC.			DELIVERY RECEIPT					REC. BY:			NAME

The format of a route card is operation-specific. Many operations begin with one type of route card and adjust it to help merchandise products more effectively. The sample above tracks products by category and sale price.

RTE	SERV #	SERV TYPE	CHANGER AMT	EMPLOYEE				MACH #	MACH DESC		MACH #
DATE		WEEK	DAY	LOCATION							RTE/SERV. #
PRODUCT											WEEK
PRICE											DAY
PAR											
FILLS											(CHECK ONE)
											REFUND
DAMAGED											CHARGE
REMOVED											C.O.D.
INVENTORY											
METER 1 READING				METER 2 READING			TESTS	REFUNDS		CASH COLLECTED	AMOUNT
CONTACT					SERV TIME	BEG	END	SLUGS	CASH COMM		
COMPANY NAME			DELIVERY RECEIPT					REC. BY:			NAME

Use the sample route card above to assist you with developing appropriate forms of your own.

Source: Midwest Vending Inc.

Machine Collection Form

Although route cards (or delivery receipts) are common in food vending, other specialties use different systems. Instead of a card, this one-page form is used to track inventory and sales for pantyhose vending.

Performed by: _____ Date: _____

Location: _____

	Slot 1 Machine 1	Slot 2 Machine 1	Slot 1 Machine 2	Slot 2 Machine 2
Color/size style				
Previous number in machine				
Number added				
New number in machine				
Money collected				
Short/over/ even				
Notes				
Total				

Source: McLean Machines & Co. Inc.

▲

when 50 percent of its products have sold. Why fill a machine when it's half-empty? As explained in Chapter 11, industry statistics show that servicing a machine when 50 percent of its products are gone minimizes the number of empty spirals and, therefore, lost sales.

In addition to minimizing empties, servicing at 50 percent (rather than 60, 70, or 80 percent) maximizes your income/expense ratio. "We strive to make at least $100 per 500-unit snack machine at every servicing," notes Wayne D. "If you merchandise correctly, you should be able to make $100 every time you open a machine."

Another way to understand these concepts is by thinking of them in terms of your local grocery store. "If a grocery store carries Charmin toilet tissue, [employees] load shelves using a space-to-sales ratio," Wayne says. "They know through their data what they need [on the shelves] every day and every week. A vending company is the same. If an operator doesn't do space-to-sales ratios, then he's continuously filling that machine."

Although operators and experts recommend relying on your distributor's statistics to start, develop your own data for each vendor as quickly as possible. Keep track of sales each time you open a machine using route cards (also called delivery receipts), such as the samples shown on page 164. For nonfood specialties, see the sample "Machine Collection Form" on page 165.

If you've computerized, as suggested in Chapter 7, transfer information from the route cards to your computer. If not, use a ledger book to track information by hand.

Still unclear about the concept of servicing machines when they're 50 percent full? We suggest you review the "On the Right Route" section in Chapter 11.

Managing Your Stash

As you may have already guessed from reviewing the "Quality Snacks Start-Up Inventory Expenses" form on page 114 in Chapter 9, within each product category you'll be stocking a variety of different items. The reason for stocking different items within each category is simple: Customers want variety.

While figuring out the right merchandising strategies on an item-by-item basis is still somewhat a matter of trial and error, a fact-based system called *category management* has begun to catch on in the vending industry. According to *Vending Times*, category management is already familiar to mass-market retailers and uses a research-based approach to stocking machines in a manner that makes the most money from the space available.

As noted by *Vending Times*, research by Nabisco Inc. says when selecting items within each category, consider each of them as belonging to one of three groups:

1. *Core.* Items that will be in every one of your machines every day; these should occupy about 20 percent of available slots.
2. *Cycle.* Items that will appear in every machine every day within specific time frames or menu cycles; these include leading consumer brands in each category

and products that present different taste profiles, as well as branded new products. These should occupy about 60 percent of machine-selling space.

3. *Choice.* "Wildcard" items placed in machines to serve requests at a given location; to improve "turns" (in other words, sales), Nabisco recommends limiting the "choice" items to three products or brands.

Again, relying on your suppliers for guidance the first time you fill your vendors, carefully tracking sales at each location allows you to fine-tune menus to appeal to the greatest number of customers.

> **Fun Fact**
> According to industry trade publication *Vending Times,* research shows that at least 20 percent of customers will walk away from a vending machine if they don't find the kind of item they want. Demand cannot be transferred to another category. In other words, a customer looking for gum will not buy a salty snack instead.

"Trusting your distributor the first time you fill is a wise idea," says DCB Consulting's Donald Blotner. "Once you build up your own information, then outside data is only helpful as a general guideline, such as when you're considering stocking a new product. For specifics, the only thing you can trust is your own numbers."

Empty Avoidance

In the real world, nothing's as simple as hypothetical examples or fact-based merchandising plans. For instance, just because a machine holds 60 units of pastries doesn't mean you will sell enough pastries every two weeks at every location to keep them from going beyond their freshness dates. To compensate, use one of the oldest tricks in the book: Fill only a portion of the slower-moving column with pastries and the balance of the column with something else.

"In locations that are slower, instead of having empties, you put something else that's a good seller at that location, such as cookies, behind," Hendersonville, Tennessee, full-line operator B.J. S. advises. "You don't walk up to any of our machines and have an empty spiral—the red light is never on. The job is pretty easy if you keep the machines pretty full."

Pulling Product

Sometimes no matter what merchandising alternatives you try, sales just aren't cutting it. In such cases, you may be faced with tough choices.

"You work with the client," emphasizes B.J. "You tell them upfront [when negotiating a contract] 'We have a minimum.' If the location doesn't reach the minimum, you sit down with the client and ask, 'Is there anything we can do? Is it the product selection? Is it us? Or is it that you have a McDonald's right outside the door?' "

▲

Bright Idea

For assistance with your first planogram, turn to a product sales representative for a major vending player, such as Nabisco Inc. Sales reps are familiar with planogramming and can quickly get you up and running.

If you dialogue with your clients, an explanation will usually become clear, B.J. says. "You need to be more price competitive, or you need to put a different selection in. Whatever it is, you try to work it out first, and then, if there's no hope, you're just going to have to pull [your vendors.] By that time, you should have made the client aware of your decision," he continues. "It's pretty tough. That's part of where being a good salesman comes in. As long as you're upfront with the client, you're most likely to develop some type of relationship, a rapport. You always hate to lose clients, but sometimes it's unavoidable."

Planning It Out

With so many variables to consider, perhaps you're wondering if there's any sort of road map that can help you reach your proper merchandising goals. Enter the ink-on-paper tool known as a planogram.

Simply stated, a planogram is a graphic display of your merchandising plan. In other words, you draw a rectangle that represents a machine, divide it up into columns according to your machine's layout, and write the names of individual items in the slots. More specifically, you place items in slots using the core, cycle, and choice columns as discussed earlier. Some operators even take it a step further.

"We have a different planogram for schools than for office buildings," comments Wayne D. "In a 20-column machine, for example, there will be 12 that are mandatory, two that are brand of the week, and six that are at the route person's discretion. Based on our sales statistics, we know what are our top 10 or 12 items are. Those 10 or 12 will be basically the same in every location."

Does this mean you need a different planogram for each machine? Not necessarily. Depending on your vending specialty, one planogram for each size of machine can be sufficient for your entire operation.

For two sample planograms that incorporate the merchandising concepts we have discussed, turn to page 170. You will also find a hypothetical snack vending company's start-up planogram on page 170.

Changing the Plan

Operators and experts suggest reviewing all your sales figures regularly and adjusting your planograms accordingly. How often you do this depends on your operation, but monthly reviews are most common.

"Variety is the life blood of vending," emphasizes broker Jim Patterson of Patterson Co. Inc. in Kenilworth, Illinois. "If the customer can memorize the machine before he goes there, the operator's in trouble because he can make a decision from his desk.

"Vending originally grew from forced coffee breaks," he continues. "But it's changing to become more customer demand-oriented, so operators need to be more sensitive to consumers' demands and wants. Even among the products that need to be there, you need to move them around. If a customer sees the same product in the same slot, they may think that it never sells and it's still there when, in fact, it's always there because it moves so well."

Like Wayne D., Patterson evokes the grocery store model. "Just like a grocery store resets the store, you need to reset the machine and move products from column to column."

Adding Excitement

In addition to the basics we've discussed, merchandising includes promoting products or concepts. For example, placing clear-plastic promotional stickers, known as "static clings," on your vendors highlights certain items. Supplied by your sales rep or your product broker, static clings can publicize a consumer contest, a single product, a particular brand, or a concept such as the ubiquitous fast-food "value meal"—buying a sandwich, side item, and a beverage.

Also available from suppliers are posters you may ask clients to display in various areas. Such posters promote individual items, the idea of purchasing from a vending machine, or the suggestion to buy a product from your machines to take home.

When it comes to contests, you can come up with your own or work with your suppliers. In vending, a contest is generally a random stickering of products in a category or column you wish to promote; the customer who buys the winning item earns a prize. Stickers can be as simple as small labels you purchase at any office supply store.

"We'll give you stickers and we'll give you T-shirts," says Patterson. "We'll provide X winning stickers and X number of prizes, such as T-shirts. Then, we either give you the prizes or list a toll-free number on the sticker that the consumer calls to redeem the prize themselves."

> **Bright Idea**
>
> Increase perceived value of "lucky sticker" contests by using your product line and wholesale pricing to your advantage. For example, if you already carry cheese popcorn, bill the contest as "one cheese popcorn per month for an entire year." Using this strategy, you won't have any unusual inventory to store and the total cost per winner would be about $2.

Category Shelf and Location Assignment

LSS Salty Snacks		LSS Salty Snacks		LSS Salty Snacks		LSS Salty Snacks		LSS Salty Snacks	
Salty Snack		Salty Snack		Salty Snack		Salty Snack		Salty Snack	
Bagged Cracker		Bagged Cookie		Salty Snack		Salty Snack		Microwave Popcorn	
Choc. Candy	Choc. Candy	Choc. Candy	Choc. Candy	Choc. Candy	Choc. Candy	Choc. Candy	Choc. Candy	Choc. Candy	Choc. Candy
Non Choc. Candy	Non Choc. Candy	Nuts	Cracker Sandwich	Cracker Sandwich	Granola Bar	Breakfast Bar	Pastry	Sleeve Cookies	Sleeve Cookies
Pastry		Pastry		Pastry		Pastry		Large Cookie	
Gum		Gum		Gum		Hard Roll Candy		Hard Roll Candy	

Salty Snacks	13
Crackers	3
Cookies	4
Chocolate Candy	10
Non Chocolate Candy	2
Nuts	1
Granola/ Breakfast Bars	2
Pastry	5
Gum	3
Hard Roll Candy	2
Total	45

Example of Core, Cycle, and Choice Product for 45-Select Machine

Fritos		Cheetos Snacks		Doritos Snacks		LSS Salty Snacks		LSS Salty Snacks	
Salty Snacks		Salty Snacks		Salty Snacks		Salty Snacks		Salty Snacks	
Bagged Crackers		Bagged Cookies		Salty Snacks		Salty Snacks Premium		Microwave Popcorn	
Reese's PBC	Snickers	M&M Peanuts	Choc. Candy	Choc. Candy	Choc. Candy	Choc. Candy	Choc. Candy	Choc. Candy	Choc. Candy
Non Choc. Candy	Non Choc. Candy	Nuts	Cracker Sandwich	Cracker Sandwich	Granola Bar	Breakfast Bar	Pastry	Oreo	Sleeve Cookies
Pastry		Pastry		Pastry		Pastry		Large Cookies	
Gum		Gum		Gum		Hard Roll Candy		Hard Roll Candy	

Core=9 spirals (20% of machine)

Cycle=28 spirals (62% of machine)

Choice=8 spirals (18% of machine)

To set up a contest yourself, affix a vending token or coupon to packages. While you won't make any cash on items purchased with the tokens, you'll encourage more usage of your machines and generate immeasurable goodwill. If you go the sticker route, you don't have to give away the farm. "We sticker items and the lucky sticker wins something like a two-liter bottle of pop," Wayne D. says.

Especially when you're new to a location, working with suppliers on cosponsoring promotions draws customers who might not otherwise use your machines. "We work with our suppliers to offer a two-for-one special on a certain type of candy bar," asserts Wayne. "And we put up signage so it's promotional for our supplier, too."

Whatever methods you use to add excitement, just do it. "It's important you don't just put product into your machine," asserts John Ochi of Vernon Hills, Illinois-based Five Star Distributors. "Spotlight it to bring it to your customers' attention."

For more clever promotional ideas, see the "Special Promotions" exhibit on page 172.

Free Vend Allure

Another way to encourage customer loyalty is placing your machines on "free vend" under given circumstances. Just as the name implies, a machine set to free vend dispenses product without requiring customers to insert any money.

Because free vend can quickly put you in the red, you'll want to work with your clients to limit the number of free vend customers. For example, your clients can use free vend during an after-hours meeting as a way to encourage and reward attendance. When the cost of a free vend is significant, a reduction in a location's commission is a common method used to offset the loss.

Couponing Arrives

The advent of the bill acceptor has provided operators with a valuable promotional opportunity that was impossible before. Because newer bill acceptors are actually small computers that read the metallic content of paper currency, they can be set to read a coupon that has an operation-specific metallic signature.

In the past, vending operators passed out coin-shaped tokens to promote usage of their machines. However, tokens are generic, which means the customer can use them in any machine. This is especially problematic when

Tip...

Smart Tip

Clients like coupons because they're easy to handle and they don't add to the payroll. Since a coupon is nonmonetary compensation, an employer can distribute them to reward performance, attendance, etc., without paying additional payroll or other taxes, and an employee isn't required to report them as taxable income.

Special Promotions

The purpose...to build a better business relationship with the clients and to move more product! Place a note on the front of the machine for special promotions or promotional-priced items. Keep holidays and the day of the week in mind for special location promotions.

Fantastic February

All candy is on sale

ONLY **35¢**

Stock Up!   Stock Up!

MMM...Muffin Monday

The Vending Company
will be bringing muffins for everyone on:
Monday, May 1st

"Thank you for your business"

Doughnuts

will be supplied **Wednesday the**
4th of July...

Courtesy of *The Vending Company.*
Thank you for your business!

PIZZA PARTY FRIDAY!

Pizza will be served
Friday, October 7th
courtesy of
The Vending Company

"It is just our way of saying THANKS!"

Win Gift Certificates

for three movie rentals
or **$10** at Denny's
or 2 tickets for the hockey game.
**Check your purchase for a
winner's sticker!**

Redeem your prize by calling
The Vending Company at 555-1234.

Win a pair of
Movie Tickets

If your purchase has the winning sticker, take it to the receptionist, and pick up your prize!

Just a special "Thank you" from
The Vending Company

TERRIFIC TUESDAY!

Ten cents for coffee

Thank you for your business, from
The Vending Company

Source: The Vending Connection

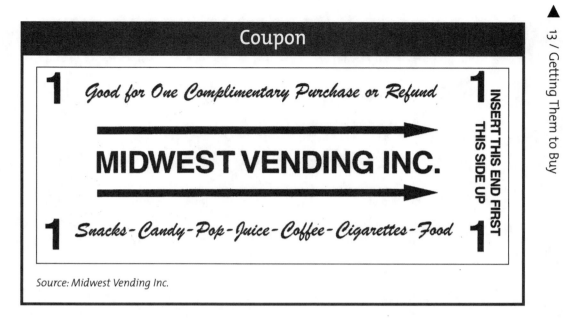

Source: Midwest Vending Inc.

more than one operation services a location, such as when you handle snacks and a bottler supplies sodas.

Although coupons cost more than tokens because bill acceptor companies charge operators for software that's needed to program a machine, according to industry magazine *Automatic Merchandiser*, the use of coupons has increased some operators' overall sales as much as 25 percent.

"We may give a client ten coupons a week or ten a quarter," says Wayne D. "The coupons allow customers to take one item, regardless of cost. In some cases, we sell the coupons to clients at a reduced cost and they use them as employee rewards or incentives, such as for meeting productivity quotas or delivery deadlines. Before, when we used the free vend system, people would take home extra items."

Coupons are also reducing refund costs significantly. As you'll learn in the next chapter, a large part of good vending customer service is providing refunds for lost coins and bills. While the most common practice is to refund in cash, nothing guarantees the cash will be reinserted into your machines. "Coupons pretty much eliminated our refund problem," Wayne says.

For more on merchandising and valuable tips related to your product specialty, be sure to contact both a general industry organization, such as the National Automatic Merchandisers Association, and groups specific to your product line, such as the International Telecard Association or the National Association of Hosiery Manufacturers.

Always Treat 'Em Right

If, as we discussed in the previous chapter, the key to attracting new accounts is a good reputation, then customer service is the key to building the reputation every successful vendor needs.

This trend is echoed in the business world at large. From the smallest start-up to the halls of corporate conglomerates, the mantra for the millennium is customer service. Once thought of only as a department, it's now considered an essential element in every corporation's culture.

Service Never Sleeps

"In the extremely competitive vending industry of today, outstanding customer service is critical to any entrepreneur's success," says industry consultant Donald Blotner of Eagan, Minnesota-based DCB Consulting. "This includes saying a cheery 'Hello' to anyone you see [when servicing machines]—not just the bosses. And saying it no matter what the circumstances—sweltering heat, bitter cold, or when you are called in to fix a machine in the middle of the night."

But customer service goes beyond that. "You have to be good with handling people, you have to resolve issues in a timely manner, and you also have to be flexible enough to make adjustments for special requests," emphasizes Blotner, a former vending operator. "If you're unfamiliar with customer service or customer service concepts, it's vital you seek training, and if you have employees, be sure they receive appropriate training as well."

From Start to Finish

For Northridge, California, full-line operator Becky P., outstanding customer service means taking the initiative to greet customers and discuss their needs. "When I walk in the [vending] room, I always say, 'Good morning, good afternoon, how's everybody?' "

As she begins servicing her machines, Becky's always on the lookout for ways to reach out. "If someone walks up to a machine next to me and makes a purchase, I always thank them. I can't tell you how many times they'll turn around and say, 'For what?' or they think I'm being sarcastic. And I'll say, 'You thank your customers. You're my customer, so I'm thanking you.'

"They don't think of it that way," she continues. "They think of the vending machine as being cold. Right then and there, you've taken that cold, inanimate machine and given it a personality. They are going to think of your smiling face and you thanking them when they make their next purchase."

The same goes for when a customer interrupts her from servicing a machine. "If a customer comes up and asks, 'Can I get something out?' my response is always 'I'd be thrilled to serve you personally' and then I hand them the item they're interested in. And then, I always, always, always thank them."

Once she's finished servicing, Becky's exit mirrors her entrance. "When I get to the door of the room, I always turn around and say, 'Goodbye. Thanks, everybody. We really appreciate you.' And it's from the heart; it's not just something I say. I truly do thank them. I understand completely that a Snickers bar is a Snickers bar, and they can go to the 7-Eleven, the AM/PM, or the catering truck, but I want them to buy it from me."

Get It Now

In addition to overt friendliness, successful operators stress the importance of prompt action on customer requests. "If a customer asks for something that's not in the machine and you have it on the truck, even if you feel like your legs are ready to fall off, you immediately go and get that [item] and bring it back to the room," Becky says. "You have made that person feel important. We all love recognition, and it's remembered."

> **Tip...**
>
> ### Smart Tip
> Whenever you're servicing machines, listen to the conversations around you. "The break room is the company grapevine," explains Northridge, California, full-line operator Becky P. "You hear if they're going to expand or if they're talking about moving to another location. Whether you're on your own or you have employees, you have to keep your ears open."

Wayne D.'s advice is the same. "Always be courteous and respond to requests for product in a timely manner. If our route driver doesn't have it on his truck, and he's not going to be there for a week, he calls the office to make sure he'll have the product the next week," says the Burnsville, Minnesota, full-line operator. "In most cases, you or your driver is there [servicing a location] an hour or an hour and a half every week," continues Wayne. "You get to know people on a first-name basis, and you get to know them fairly well."

Bearing the Brunt

In the real world, your customer interactions won't always be happy. "[Sometimes] I'll walk in the room and immediately someone may be like 'Da, da, da, da, da,' " says Becky, imitating a machine gun. "I say, 'I've given you the respect to say good morning to you. I'm going to handle whatever the problem is, but I need you to smile and say good morning to me.' That immediately defuses the situation because nine out of ten times, the frustration and anger really isn't at you; it's at something that's happened at work."

Knowing a little about psychology goes a long way in the vending business, stresses Becky. "Vending does get the brunt of a lot of things," she says, laughing. "Sometimes that kick mark [on a machine] is because a guy just got chewed out by his supervisor. So you have to let people vent sometimes. But—and there have been tons of articles written on this—as long as they know you'll handle a complaint or a problem right away, 98 percent of your customers will be satisfied and come back. If you blow them off, you've lost that customer."

Even enduring a regular whiner can make a difference in an operator's success. "You will have the perpetual complainer," Becky admits. "They're just looking for attention because the only attention they ever got in life was through negativity. When my [route] guys say, 'Sam is such pain. He complains every day,' I ask, 'Is he buying every day?' And he'll say, 'Yeah, but he complains every day.' I reply, 'Listen to him. Listen to him. He's looking for attention.' Again, this is where the psychology of dealing with people comes in. If you have complaints, it's very important to listen [to them]."

Special Requests

Invariably someone's going to ask you to stock an item regularly for them. Whether or not you do is a judgment call.

"If two or three people end up buying an item every day, then we make a lot of money," comments Wayne D. "Generally, in a snack machine, there's enough room to add a special request. When they get those special requests, people who say they will purchase the product usually end up buying it. We don't have the problem that people request something and don't purchase it."

However, at some point you're likely to be faced with a tough choice, regardless of purchasing frequency or profitability. "If the key executive at a location drinks Diet Dr Pepper, then we put it in," acknowledges Wayne. "If [the person is] your vending contact, you have no choice but to leave it in. And even if we change personnel, there's a note on the inside of the machine or on the route card [stating the preference]."

If you're forced to stock a money-loser in order to profit overall, there's still a way to minimize the damage, Wayne says. Simply stock such products in a column that holds fewer items, or place them in a column that—for whatever reason—is slow no matter what you attempt to sell.

In some vending specialties, you'll have other alternatives to saying "no." For example, in telecards and pantyhose, successful entrepreneurs say you can offer to sell special products direct. "Sometimes [when I'm loading machines] customers tell me, 'The queen size [pantyhose] aren't big enough. Do you have any queen XXs?' " says Baltimore operator Janice M. When she can't stock a particular product she replies, "I have a catalog, and you can buy them directly from me."

"I like the fact that they realize they can just come up to me, and they can tell me what they

> **Beware!**
> Just because a customer requests and purchases a product doesn't mean you should overlook that item's profitability—or lack thereof. "It's important to stay on top of unit costs," Northridge, California, full-line operator Becky P. stresses. "Otherwise, before you know it, you could be losing one or two cents on that product, and that adds up at the end of the year."

think and what they want—what works for them and what doesn't work," she continues. "And they know that I'll try to resolve it. I think that's great, because when you start losing touch with your customers, that's when you start losing your customers. My mom and dad had a store and they always talked to a customer who had a complaint; they never said, 'I'm too busy.' I learned that from them."

Drawing the Line

There is a point where successful vendors draw the special request line. "I won't carry card issuers that are fly-by-nights," emphasizes Preston, Washington, telecard operator Pat W. "I've got a request right now for a rate, but I can't find a reputable card issuer. I can get within a cent and a half."

Since she can usually find an alternative, she's now in uncharted waters. "I'll have to tell the client that I won't do business with a nonreputable card issuer," Pat says. "I've never had this situation, so I don't know what's going to happen. He may sell the card he wants over the counter, and it'll take business away from me. If so, I'll have to take his machine out."

I Want a Refund

Not surprisingly, another common customer request is for a refund. To which most operators respond similarly to Becky P. "Our philosophy is 'If you're not happy, you can have your money back.' For example, a sandwich may be perfectly good," says Becky. "But if they didn't like it, our response is, 'Would you like another sandwich or would you like your money back?' If they say, 'It was spoiled,' we ask, 'Would you like your money and another item?' "

The reason for such generosity despite tight profit margins is simple. "It's not the $2 sandwich that you lost," Becky explains. "It's the fact that chances are they spend anywhere from a dollar to five or six dollars a day [on your products], and if you lose that day in and day out, five or six days a week, that adds up at the end of the year. Yes, there are those who will abuse [our refund policy]. But it's like the big retail stores—the percentage [of those who abuse it] in the long run is small."

In fact, Becky claims a liberal refund policy not only discourages abuse but also helps her make product improvements. "Once people learn that they don't have to make up stories

> **Beware!**
> Sometimes you'll need extra acumen for evaluating complaints. "The wife of one of my clients kept telling him that she couldn't use my cards," recounts Preston, Washington, telecard vendor Pat W. "So I [called the issuer for] printouts, which showed the calls she was making. [It turned out that my client] had a marriage problem, not a card problem."

and that you're going to take care of them, it doesn't get abused. Lots of times they'll even come up [to us] and say, 'Find out if your commissary changed their mayonnaise because it's just a little off; it's not tasting right,' " she continues. "I'll call up [the supplier] and they'll say, 'You're right, we did go with another one, and you're the fourth call today. I'm not going to use this stuff anymore because people don't like it.' So this kind of communication with your customers and your suppliers is very important. When your customer knows you're approachable, it keeps things running well."

What Have You Learned, Dorothy?

If you are vending a pricey product, such as telecards, you will need a more sophisticated refund policy because your costs are so much higher than in food vending.

"One of the biggest mistakes I made was taking back cards without calling [the card issuer's] customer service first," Pat W. recounts. Since her locations are primarily convenience 'stores, the problem was that angry customers would raise a ruckus, and merchants would hand them a refund to quiet them down. Because the face values of her cards are $5, $10, or $20, refunds could quickly put Pat's business in the red.

After getting caught with almost $200 in refunds one month, she decided enough was enough. "I told my merchants to refer [refund requests] to me unless it's someone they knew personally," says Pat. She instructed merchants to give out her contact information or take down the customer's name and number and give it to her to follow up.

Usually, the issue has nothing to do with evil intentions. "Most often, people are dialing the number incorrectly, or they scratched the coating over the PIN number too hard and the PIN number came off," explains Pat. To solve the former, Pat teaches the customer how to use the card properly. For the latter, she calls the card issuer to obtain a new PIN number.

In some cases, the card or card issuer is at fault. "If someone says they've been overcharged, then I'll call the card issuer," Pat says. "Many times there are computer glitches, particularly with calls to Third World countries, and the card issuer will put money back on the card."

But computer glitches aren't the only source of overcharges. "Some companies randomly 'double bong' [charge a duplicate connection fee] a number of cards in a given batch. Most of the time, customers don't notice. But my customers watch. If I find out that [double bonging] is happening, I don't darken [that card issuer's] door again."

As we discussed in Chapter 9, for high-end specialty products such as telecards, your best defense is a good offense. Researching and selecting reputable products is key. "Less than .01 percent of the cards come back with a complaint," asserts Pat.

But It Was Jammed

In addition to bad product, many refund requests stem from real or imagined coin and bill acceptor jams. In nonpublic locations catering to employees, such as offices and factories, most operators handle this situation with a refund slip system.

An envelope or similar container, such as a plastic bag, marked 'blank refund slips' is mounted on the side of one of the vending machines. Another envelope, marked 'completed refund slips' is mounted next to the blank slip envelope. The next time machines are serviced, completed slips are collected. The appropriate amount of money owed a customer is placed in a regular business envelope, sealed, and the name of the person is written on the front. Refunds are then given to the location's contact person or a designated individual, such as a receptionist, to distribute.

Alternatively, a stash of coins and bills are provided to a certain individual, again the contact person or other designated person. In this case, the designated individual collects slips and hands out refunds immediately.

The second scenario is the preferred method. "You want to alleviate frustration by taking care of their problem immediately," emphasizes Becky P. "The best way to do that is to find someone who's willing to do an immediate refund bank so your customers can get their money back right away. You give the refund bank person a zippered pouch with $10 in change. Although $10 is plenty, if they want $15, give it to them."

You can often enlist those who handle your refund bank to disseminate change for larger bills, Becky says. "I know I used to do that as a courtesy for my employees when I worked in manufacturing, but not everyone wants to be responsible for [making change], so you just ask."

Whatever system you employ, use the refund slips for more than just proper bookkeeping. "Read your refund slips," admonishes Becky. "They tell you something. If you have lots of refunds on 'Crunchy Pretzels,' then you probably have a coin-mech problem."

And refund money as soon as possible. "Do it the next time you are at the stop," Becky advises "That way the people know they are going to get their money back. This is very, very important—some people will go ballistic over a nickel, because that is the last frustration [they can handle] for the day."

Refund slips need not be elaborate or expensive. Necessary elements are space for the customer's name, refund amount, and reason for the refund. Including the name of your company on the slip visually

Dollar Stretcher

If you're computerized, you can create refund slips on your computer and print out or photocopy them in quantity.

Refund Slip

A Matter of Taste
Refund Slip

Print Name:

Date: _____   Item: _____

Location: _____   Amount: _____

Machine: _____   Reason: _____

This information is important so that we may improve our services. Thank you!

reinforces your commitment to customer service and reassures the customer they're filling out the right form. For an example, see the "Refund Slip" above.

Public Offerings

If your locations are open to the public, your refund system will more likely rely on telecommunications rather than pencil and paper. Prominently affixing your company name and telephone number is key.

"I want people to be able to contact me for things like [losing their money]," says Janice M. Although she lists her business telephone number on her machines, her voice greeting encourages callers to contact her via pager.

An issue for refunding money from public vendors has always been lack of guaranteed reinsertions. Wayne D., who serves park and recreational facilities, discovered from the statistics he keeps that refund customers often were not plugging the money back into his machines.

With the advent of advanced electronic bill and coin acceptors, he's now solved the problem by giving free item coupons to those who call for their money back. "We really prefer [coupons], because we know they're using the product." This also assists in cases where Wayne is not the only operator serving a nonpublic location. "If we're sharing the location with a bottler, then [we know] they won't use the refund on the bottler."

For a detailed explanation of how couponing works, see Chapter 13.

If It's Broken, Fix It

Whether tied to a specific refund request or the result of watching your refund slips, you will be called on to repair your vendors. "When people call for an out-of-service machine, they want it fixed now," Wayne points out. "If you can't respond quickly enough, you'll have lost sales and dissatisfied customers."

As we discussed in Chapter 2, your challenge with daytime emergencies is balancing the negative impact of the outage with the effect of delaying finishing the rest of your route to repair it. While your decision may vary with the circumstances, always provide clients and customers with your best estimate of when you'll be there.

Smart Tip

Tip...

It's a fact: Customers who receive voice mail when there's a problem are less satisfied than those who reach a person. Start-ups without any employees solve this problem by carrying a cellular phone, which can double as your business line.

"Our overall service turnarounds are logged on the computer," notes Hendersonville, Tennessee, full-line operator B.J. S., whose operation includes two full-time service technicians. "We log from the time of the report to the time it was fixed. Our average is 47 minutes. And if somebody wants me to guarantee it, then I do, which is why we factor in travel time."

During off-hours, expect customers to insist on quick action. "If you're working a night shift and you go to a machine and it's not working, you want it fixed," says Becky P. "It's holidays, Saturdays, and Sundays. We may be in our pajamas, but we throw on our sweats and take care of the call."

To reduce emergencies, successful operators and industry experts stress preventative maintenance, paying attention to refund slip trends and, for the computerized, tracking coin-to-bill ratios to spot fluctuations. For more on time- and money-saving tips, see Chapter 8.

Ask What They Want

Although we've spent a great deal of time discussing managing machine outages, handling product complaints, and giving refunds, an equally important customer service task is designing some preemptive strikes. Key to reducing griping on the back end is asking for customer input upfront.

"We survey locations to find out what they want," comments Wayne D. "If what's requested is off-the-wall, we can't do that. If it's within reason, we will. For instance, if two or three people request a [specific name-brand soda], then we put it in the machine."

To get the most from her survey efforts, Janice M. includes both quality of service questions as well as product selection questions on index-card sized questionnaires she places inside her hosiery boxes. "It wasn't long after I started [the business] that I

Smart Tip

To be profitable in today's competitive vending market, know your customers better than they know themselves, says the comprehensive report *The Future of the Vending and Foodservice Industry 1998–2013*, commissioned by the National Automatic Merchandising Association. The report states: "Only if you do can you add the value necessary to differentiate yourself [from competitors] in your customer's eyes."

began including customer comment cards because it was the only way I could find out what people really wanted," she says. "At first, it was just a small card I printed myself—the same as the ones you use to print business cards on your computer."

As her business grew, she turned to a professional printer. "Now it is a two-sided card," notes Janice. "I have always put size, color, and style (such as Lycra or micro-fiber). But now it is a little more complicated because I have more things to offer."

Whether your business lends itself to a comment card or the more standard sheet-of-paper survey, follow Janice's lead by distributing a questionnaire that provides you with both service and product feedback. Using a dual-purpose form provides you with the maximum amount of information for a minimum amount of effort. For an example of a detailed form that you can adapt to fit your business's needs, see the "At-Location Survey of Customer Reactions" on page 188.

Electronic a Plus

Another way to encourage feedback is to get on the Internet. As we discussed in Chapter 12, using the Internet as a marketing tool has yet to catch on in the vending industry. But what's more important is that your customers have likely learned that e-mail is a far more efficient communications mechanism than voice mail.

Recent surveys show Internet use by firms with fewer than 200 employees is far exceeding the expected adoption rate. Thirty-two percent already use the Web for purchasing and 30 percent for selling. Businesses are realizing that the Internet is a customer service tool as well.

One of the ways you can quickly differentiate yourself from all the rest is, at minimum, by offering to do business by e-mail. And if you're even remotely computer-inclined, software that automatically comes with new computer systems often includes easy ways to build a simple but professional Web site.

For a more detailed discussion of Internet affairs, see Chapter 12 in this book.

Make Yourself Available

Whether it is in person, by phone, or via cyberspace, the customer service bottom line is being accessible. Savvy entrepreneurs know this goes beyond giving your main contact your business card.

"When I go to put a vendor in, I get the manager and the clerks who are standing around," Pat W. says. After teaching them telecard basics, she answers any questions they might have. "Then I give them each a business card and five extra business cards and tell them to put them everywhere. And I tell them to contact me day or night."

> ### Dollar Stretcher
>
> As competition for telephone customers heats up, many local and long-distance carriers offer Internet access in combination with other services and at a reduced cost.

Going the Extra Mile

Operators who serve special populations may find their situation requires going beyond the tried-and-true customer service techniques we've discussed here. Becky P.'s solution to ethnic diversity and non-English-speaking customers is a model for any operator, regardless of their vending specialty.

"Some employees can't read and write in their own language. How can we expect them to read menu boards or vending machine instructions in our language?" questions Becky. "Because there are so many people in our area speaking different languages, we've had to develop a unique approach to serving our vending customers."

After placing machines, Becky holds training sessions with non-English-speaking employees. Using a bilingual interpreter, she personally teaches employees how to put

---

Get Personal

In closed, nonpublic locations, such as offices and manufacturing facilities, being personally involved in employee affairs is another way to encourage buying. "We get involved by bringing complimentary desserts and beverages to employee functions," says Northridge, California, full-line operator Becky P. The birth of a baby? "We bring them baby toys."

Once, after the death of an employee's family member, co-workers held a potluck lunch to help raise money for the funeral expenses. Becky brought in complimentary desserts and joined in on the fund-raiser, including staying for the meal. "Our customers are very generous. If one doesn't have food to eat, they all pitch in to help."

It's that generous, energetic attitude of her customers that Becky's operation thrives on. "We feel vending is a benefit for employees. We also understand the morale of the lunchroom. If we can help make our customer's lunch break a more positive one, we do everything we can."

---

money into each machine and how to retrieve products. "Nobody wants to be thought of as incompetent. Our goal is to have our customers walk up to a vending machine with confidence and treat the machines with [respect]."

Sessions may take two days or two weeks, depending on the number of employees and their knowledge of vendors. But Becky doesn't stop there. Whenever a new machine is introduced, more sessions are scheduled. Often ongoing training sessions are even necessary because many manufacturing plants depend on high-turnover temporary labor.

Beyond Training Sessions

Along with training non-English-speaking employees, Becky also provides appropriate vendors. "Labels on vendors (particularly canned drink machines) are intimidating if you can't read them," she asserts. Therefore, Becky insists all her machines, including canned beverages, have glass fronts. "People know what they like. They can recognize the product if they see the package—they just can't read the label."

Because those unfamiliar with a language often require a few more moments to make selections, Becky frequently encourages management to stagger break times. "Staggering breaks by just five minutes allows the first group of employees enough time to purchase their drinks and move on to the snack machine before the next group arrives."

The ethnic diversity of her customers requires Becky to take a personalized approach for each account. Because of the large mix of cultures, which differs greatly even within the same account, what works in one machine doesn't work in another. "There are no cookie-cutter machines in our accounts," she stresses.

Becky has also gone out of her way to fulfill customers' special requests, often shopping for requested items on a moment's notice. Says Becky, "I go to the local wholesale club several times a week to pick up a product a customer has requested."

Old-Fashioned Service in a Modern World

Becky contends it's still possible in today's world to take care of the customer the old-fashioned way—with exceptional service—while still making a profit. Once the language barrier is broken, the cultural diversity of her customers gives Becky additional opportunities to differentiate herself from her competition by providing a wide range of products and services.

Still, she admits, it takes some creative thinking. "Our clients have asked us not to get institutionalized with our company. They worry that if we do, they won't receive the personal service we give them now." But she's quick to add that she has no intention of sacrificing her customer-centered orientation. "We're still growing, learning, and having fun."

At-Location Survey of Customer Reactions

XYZ Vending Company
Customer Questionnaire

We're doing a survey of what our customers think about vending machines and about the vending service at this location.

1. Have you used the vending machines here in the past two weeks? (Check one answer)

   ❑ Yes (Go on to question 2)

   ❑ No: If no, why not? (Skip to question 3)

2. (If Yes to question 1) In the past two weeks, how many times have you purchased the following products from a vending machine here? (Circle one code for each item below)

Coffee or hot drink	0	1	2	3	4	5	6	7	8	9	10+
Soft drinks	0	1	2	3	4	5	6	7	8	9	10+
Juice	0	1	2	3	4	5	6	7	8	9	10+
Sandwich or salad	0	1	2	3	4	5	6	7	8	9	10+
Fruit, yogurt, etc	0	1	2	3	4	5	6	7	8	9	10+
Candy, gum, or snacks	0	1	2	3	4	5	6	7	8	9	10+
Milk or ice cream	0	1	2	3	4	5	6	7	8	9	10+

3. I will read you some statements about the vending machines at this location. Ask first whether the person agrees or disagrees—after telling you which, ask "agree strongly"? or "agree somewhat"?—or "disagree strongly"? or "disagree somewhat"?

Product	Agree		Disagree		
	Strongly	Somewhat	Somewhat	Strongly	No Answer
a. Most of the time I can find a sufficient variety of products in each machine. (Do you agree with that statement, or disagree with that statement? Agree strongly, or agree somewhat, disagree strongly, or disagree somewhat?)	4	3	2	1	0
b. I would rather buy brand-name products than a nonbrand item.	4	3	2	1	0
c. Products in our machines usually are fresh.	4	3	2	1	0
d. The quality of the products in our machines is as good as the same products in other retail outlets.	4	3	2	1	0

At-Location Survey of Customer Reactions, continued

Product	Agree Strongly	Agree Somewhat	Disagree Somewhat	Disagree Strongly	No Answer
e. Prices in these machines are, for the most part, reasonable.	4	3	2	1	O
f. The product I want is seldom sold out when I get to the machine.	4	3	2	1	O
g. I like the coffee from our machine.	4	3	2	1	O
h. I would prefer to have a larger selection of soft drinks.	4	3	2	1	O

Machines

	Agree Strongly	Agree Somewhat	Disagree Somewhat	Disagree Strongly	No Answer
i. The vending machines here are easy to operate.	4	3	2	1	O
j. If I don't have enough change, it's still pretty easy to use the machines.	4	3	2	1	O
k. The machines are usually neat and clean.	4	3	2	1	O
l. I wish we had more machines at this location.	4	3	2	1	O
m. The machines at this location are seldom out of order.	4	3	2	1	O

Service

	Agree Strongly	Agree Somewhat	Disagree Somewhat	Disagree Strongly	No Answer
n. The people who service our machines are usually friendly and courteous.	4	3	2	1	O
o. It's easy to get refunds when something is wrong.	4	3	2	1	O
p. During the past four weeks I've had no problems with the machines.	4	3	2	1	O
q. The machines at this location are serviced at least every two days.	4	3	2	1	O

Company Identity

	Agree Strongly	Agree Somewhat	Disagree Somewhat	Disagree Strongly	No Answer
r. I have no idea who owns and operates the machines at this facility.	4	3	2	1	O
s. The company that services them seems to care about its customers.	4	3	2	1	O

▲

At-Location Survey of Customer Reactions, continued

t. The name of the company that owns and services the machines here is:

_____

(write name as given)

❑ Don't know the name (check here)

4. Now I would like to ask your opinion about the products being offered. Tell me which products you'd like to see offered in the machines besides what's available now.

1. _____ 2. _____ 3. _____

4. _____ 5. _____ 6. _____

5. Which of the following products do you feel are reasonably priced? (Check All That Apply)

❑ Hot Beverages　　❑ Soft drinks　　❑ Candy　　❑ Snacks

❑ Sandwiches　　❑ Salads　　❑ Milk　　❑ Juices　　❑ Cigarettes

6. I'd like to ask you a few questions about yourself so we will be able to classify your answers according to the different groups of people we're talking to...

a. Sex:　　❑ Male　　❑ Female

b. Age:　　❑ Under 18　　❑ 18–24　　❑ 25–34　　❑ 35–44　　❑ 45–55　　❑ Over 55

c. Occupation: _____

d. If this is an employer area, or a school, how long have you worked here (or gone to school here?) _____ Years.

How to Score and Total the Responses

The questionnaire statements are weighted: 4=agree strongly; 3=agree somewhat; 2=disagree somewhat; 1=disagree strongly; 0=don't know/no answer.

1. For each separate statement multiply each of the four numbers (1-4) times the number of responses each number received.

2. Add up the result of the four multiplications.

3. Divide the sum by the total number of questions answered on this segment (including the "0"-no answer responses.)

This will give you the score of responses on the scale from 1 to 4 (for example, 2.94 means "on average people tend to agree somewhat.")

Source: National Automatic Merchandising Association

Monitoring
Progress

Throughout this book, you've heard successful vending entrepreneurs emphasize the importance of a certain aspect of running a profitable company that many small-businesses owners love to hate: managing your finances. Luckily, for vending entrepreneurs the process is uncomplicated, and there are plenty of tools out there to help.

▲

Perhaps you're wondering why you need to crunch more numbers in the first place. After all, you already tackled the math in Chapter 6. The answer: That chapter covered what you need to begin. Once you're up and running, you'll want to periodically make sure your business is on a healthy track.

As someone with a bird's-eye view of vending operations notes, 15 to 20 percent of vending businesses that purchase from his company are bankrupt without even knowing it. "They don't watch the p's and q's of the economics. Just because you have cash flow doesn't mean you're in the black," says John Ochi of Vernon Hills, Illinois-based Five Star Distributors. How does he know? "When people apply for credit [with us], we get a glimpse of their financial picture. Sometimes it just blows us away."

This doesn't mean your financial checkups have to be painful. Since you are armed with all the valuable tips in this book, your reports may demonstrate just what a savvy entrepreneur you are—maybe even more so than you expected. But if the numbers are below par, regular monitoring will give you plenty of time to make adjustments and save your business from failure.

It's All in the Tools

The primary accounting tool you'll use to track your progress is an income and expense statement, also referred to as a profit and loss statement (or P&L), which basically organizes your collections and disbursements for a specific period of time. Generally, businesses generate monthly income and expense reports as well as quarterly or annual summaries.

A monthly report gives you a snapshot of the current period but doesn't show you whether the strong months outweigh the weak ones overall. By adding up the months quarterly or annually, you'll see whether you're making the profits you desire or if adjustments need to be made.

While some operators still do this work by hand, tracking your income and expenses is a good example of where a computer can be a real timesaver. Not only do popular personal finance programs such as QuickBooks add up the numbers for you, they typically use a checkbook-style on-screen metaphor to make entering information as easy as writing it down in your checkbook register. You don't need to know anything about accounting or report generation; the software does it for you. The software will also calculate commissions you owe to a location automatically, giving you more time for your main income-producing activity: servicing your machines.

Making a Statement

To bring the issue down to earth, check out the income and expense statements on pages 194 and 196 of the two hypothetical vending companies, Quality Snacks and QuickCard, we've been following throughout this book. Both are start-up, part-time, homebased operations. Quality Snacks maintains 15 snack machines, all with the same capacity, while QuickCard services ten machines, five with two columns and five with four columns.

Quality Snacks' sales average $160 per machine per week. QuickCard's weekly sales are 25 $5 cards, 75 $10 cards, and 50 $20 cards. Inventory cost calculations for these businesses can be found in Chapter 9 on page 114. The balance of the income and expense figures have been drawn from the operators we interviewed and industry statistics.

You will notice nearly every line item on the statement has an expense for the

Dollar Stretcher

Today's operators view computers as a savings, not an expense. "Previously, operators spent thousands of dollars on machines and trucks, but they wouldn't spend it on managing the business," notes Jim Patterson of Kenilworth, Illinois-based product brokerage Patterson Co. Inc. "Software helps you [figure out] how often you're at a particular location, manage your machine throughput, organize your route structures, and so much more."

month. This is because it's customary to prorate expenses paid annually, semiannually, or quarterly to more accurately reflect the net profit or loss for the month. For example, "Subscriptions/dues" includes membership in each respective company's industry association. These dues are paid annually, so for the purposes of each income and expense statement, the dues have been divided by 12.

After the statements for Quality Snacks and QuickCard, you'll find a blank income and expense statement worksheet on page 202. Although an income and expense statement can either be very detailed—breaking down line items into subcategories— or general—combining many subcategories into larger categories—we've provided you with the basic line items you'll need to get up to speed, fast.

On the Machine's Level

In addition to tracking your business' overall income and expenses, use the same formats we've presented here to monitor each vending location. Otherwise, how will you know if a location is holding its own, going gangbusters, or falling on its face? "You need to look at every location as a profit center," explains veteran start-up watcher Vince Gumma of Chicago-based equipment distributor American Vending Sales. "Keep a P&L on each of them and not overall."

To track income and expense information by location, many of the line items will have to be prorated. To do this, just calculate the percentage of total gross sales each location represents. Use the location's percentage to allocate a portion of each general expense. Of course you will not prorate three key line items—income, product costs, and sales taxes—because they are specific to each location. Instead, assign the exact

Quality Snacks Income and Expense Statement

Below is an income and expense statement for our hypothetical snack food operator, Quality Snacks. For a description of Quality Snacks, see Chapter 6.

For July 200x

Income	
Machine sales	$9,600.00
Other sales	N/A
Total Monthly Income	**$9,600.00**
Expenses	
Advertising/marketing	17.50
Commissions	960.00
CPA/accounting	20.00
Depreciation	432.00
Office equipment/furnishings	48.00
Vehicles	N/A
Vendors	384.00
Insurance	100.00
Licenses and fees	50.00
Office expenses	260.30
Office supplies	20.30
Rent*	100.00
Repairs/maintenance	20.00
Telephone	80.00
Utilities*	30.00
Payroll**	0

Quality Snacks Income and Expense Statement, continued

Product Expenses	5,000.00
Cost of goods sold	4,800.00
Product loss	200.00
Professional services***	25.00
Sales/use taxes	768.00
Subscriptions/dues	22.50
Travel, meals, entertainment	0
Vehicle expenses	750.00
Lease payments	500.00
Maintenance and repair	250.00
Vending equipment expenses	894.20
Machine purchases	825.00
Parts and repairs	19.20
Delivery/moving/freight	50.00
Other miscellaneous expenses	25.75
Total Expenses	**$9,315.25**
Net monthly profit (loss) before taxes	$284.75
Income tax (estimated)	$31.06
Net monthly profit (loss) after taxes	$253.69

*portion of household expense allocated to the business
**The owner of Quality Snacks does not draw a salary, relying instead on a percentage of net profits for income.
***includes contract labor

QuickCard Income and Expense Statement

Below is an income and expense statement for our hypothetical telecard oper-ator, QuickCard. For a description of QuickCard, see Chapter 6.

For July 200x	
Income	
Machine sales	9,375.00
Other sales	100.00
Total Monthly Income	**9,475.00**
Expenses	
Advertising/marketing	10.00
Commissions	1,895.00
CPA/accounting	0.00
Depreciation	246.36
Office equipment/furnishings	9.48
Vehicles	47.38
Vendors	189.50
Insurance	45.00
Licenses and fees	7.00
Office expenses	150.30
Office supplies	10.30
Rent*	75.00
Repairs/maintenance	5.00
Telephone	45.00
Utilities*	15.00
Payroll**	0

QuickCard Income and Expense Statement, continued

Product Expenses	**5,884.50**
Cost of goods sold	5,874.50
Product loss	10.00
Professional services***	30.00
Sales/use taxes	663.25
Subscriptions/dues	18.00
Travel, meals, entertainment	0
Vehicle expenses	50.00
Lease payment	N/A
Maintenance and repair	50.00
Vending equipment expenses	301.00
Machine loans (three 4-column)	246.00
Parts and repairs	5.00
Delivery/moving/freight	50.00
Other miscellaneous expenses	0
Total Expenses	**$9,300.41**
Net monthly profit (loss) before taxes	$174.59
Income tax (estimated)	$19.74
Net monthly profit (loss) after taxes	$154.85

*portion of household expense allocated to the business
**The owner of QuickCard does not draw a salary, relying instead on a percentage of net profits for income.
***includes contract labor

income and product costs generated by a location to that location. That way, you will know which locations are making a profit and which ones need fine-tuning.

For more on turning an underachiever around, see Chapter 13.

High-Tech or Low-Tech?

If you're purchasing an existing organization with a sizable number of machines, you may want to collect data with handheld computers. These nifty palmsized devices are customized to your operation and replace paper route cards. Drivers punch in numbers and upon returning to the shop, the data automatically downloads into the appropriate slots in your accounting software.

While this new technology proposes to replace the time-honored route card system, one operator suggests studying the technology more carefully before making the investment. "My concern when I took over was accountability and safeguards," says Hendersonville, Tennessee, full-line operator B.J. S., who purchased his business from his father-in-law. "There were no checkpoints. They weren't even tracking the counters on the machines. It was all on the honor system."

To turn what he discovered was a nearly floundering business around, B.J. decided to try the new technology. "At the time, I believed I needed to keep track of every item and every penny. Computerization was the only way to do this because of the manual cost otherwise. Besides, I thought [initiating a manual sytem] would be traveling backwards."

Although he tried the handheld system for a while, he eventually abandoned it for a variety of reasons. Route drivers found the handhelds difficult to operate. In addition, employees became frustrated when the handhelds malfunctioned, particularly in the heat of the summer. Now, some of B.J.'s drivers continue to use their handhelds, but most have been switched back to the route card system. "I think you're better off to have a good inventory control in your warehouse, review your meter readings, and inventory your trucks regularly. Your key number is cost of goods sold: If someone is stealing product, it will go up. We check [cost of goods sold] once a month for changes of more than plus or minus one-half of a percent."

Smart Tip

Tip...

Whenever you are considering an investment in advanced technology, locate an operation outside your competition area that's already implemented it. The industry organization for your vending specialty can help. Then, pay a visit to the site and see how things really work. Your time investment and travel expenses will be minimal compared to what it would cost you to buy an inappropriate technology that you eventually abandon.

Ode to Depreciation

Regardless of how you keep your data, a commonly overlooked line item is depreciation. Because it's not something you actually pay out, it's easy to miss the importance of tracking this expense. By putting depreciation on your income and expense statements, you'll see how much money you need to put aside each year. This ensures funds will be available when it's time to purchase new equipment.

"It isn't just buying a machine and putting it out there," Burnsville, Minnesota, full-line operator Wayne D. emphasizes. "It depreciates. If you don't put money aside [to compensate], the machine is going to depreciate to nothing and be worth nothing. Personally, I believe it's the biggest pitfall of being in business—if you live off of depreciation [instead of putting money aside], you're never going to get ahead."

Not surprisingly, depreciation calculations can be complicated, which is where your accounting software or an accounting professional comes in. Either one can set up the appropriate equations for you, and all you have to do is plug the numbers in.

> ### Dollar Stretcher
>
> Although you'll want to set aside funds each month to save for when your machines need replacing, you may take a tax write-off for a significant portion, or sometimes all, of your equipment purchases in the same year as you buy the equipment. This is called a Section 179 deduction. Contact the IRS for more information at (800) 829-1040.

Taxing Questions

Talking about depreciation almost always leads to the subject of taxes, so now's as good a time as any to cover what a vending entrepreneur needs to know.

First, organized documentation is your friend. While the IRS watches every business, they scrutinize homebased ones even more. If the standard form letter with the "a" word in it (audit) comes to your door, the more documentation you have and the more organized you are, the better.

Even though you are not required to keep receipts below a certain amount, when you are sitting at your auditor's desk, you will wish you had. And it can all be so easy. Just make up some file folders for each line item on your income and expense statement. Then pop receipts inside. When you purchase with a credit card, simply staple receipts to the statement when it arrives.

> ### Fun Fact
>
> Perhaps the burden of the IRS, like everything else in life, is relative. "The tax situation in this country is a joke," says Sweden native B.J. S., a Hendersonville, Tennessee, full-line operator. "I'm used to paying 60 percent in taxes."

> **Beware!**
>
> Remember that as a business owner, you no longer have an employer who deducts taxes from your paycheck. If your operation nets more than $400 annually, you'll be liable for Social Security and Medicare to the tune of almost 15 percent. Avoid a whopping surprise on April 15 by calculating your estimated taxes every month on your income and expense statements.

This advice goes for sales as well as income tax. As a retailer, you are subject to both. But since you are not making face-to-face sales, your customers pay sales taxes as part of the product price. Thus, computing the sales tax you owe amounts to multiplying your gross sales by the sales tax percentage.

While sales tax laws vary by locality, you're likely to be required to factor in any items you purchased for resale but were consumed by you or someone else. Hence, if you donate products to an organization or eat a candy bar everyday from your inventory, you'll be required to add in their retail value before computing your tax.

Because your sales taxes are less obvious than for businesses that can charge them separately on an invoice or a receipt, a pitfall for many start-ups is failing to put the tax money they owe aside. By tracking sales taxes as a separate line item on your income and expense statements, the total you owe will never be a surprise.

In general, you also want to watch that your tax-deductible expenses and cost of items consumed are about the same as any other vending business of your size and type. While local and federal tax agencies audit a certain percentage of taxpayers randomly, those with numbers outside the norm automatically trigger red flags in computers and get tagged for closer scrutiny.

Finally, if the whole issue of taxes and record-keeping makes you squirm, consulting an accountant now can save you a bundle of headaches, not to mention dough, later on.

Be sure to review Chapter 7 for home-office deduction tips. Other good resources are Entrepreneur's business start-up guides *Starting & Running Your Homebased Business* and *Growing Your Business*. For information on the latter two options, see the Appendix.

Eggs in Many Baskets

Monitoring the progress of your business is also about managing its growth. While it's logical to conclude the more anchor accounts you have, the better off you are, what's really key is diversity.

"Never put all your eggs in one basket," Wayne D. admonishes. "We make sure no one dominates any segment of our market. You can start with one big client as long as you have safeguards or contracts. Then you'd best make that client a smaller part of your business as soon as possible."

Another common pitfall is growing in tandem with an anchor client. "It's easy to fall into that trap no matter what size you are," says Wayne. As the client grows, your profits will increase along with your investment in new vendors and, for some, employees. The problem comes when that company decides to downsize, relocate, or allow most of its staff to telecommute. "Ultimately, if you lose a third of your business, you'll still have the overhead."

To distribute your eggs properly, always be conscious of expanding your business. "A vending business is something you continually have to grow," says Vince Gumma of Vernon Hills, Illinois-based American Vending Sales. "I see people who get into it and plateau. They don't want to get bigger, and pretty soon they're getting smaller and they don't know why. Remember, you're going to lose locations eventually—nothing is forever."

Like too much of any good thing, too much growth too fast should also be avoided. "One of the most common mistakes I see is overextending oneself," notes Five Star Distributors' Ochi. "That is, growing too quickly without understanding your financial wherewithal and expecting your distributor to bail you out. Now that the industry is mature, we're not as inclined to take chances on operators who aren't good business managers."

Income and Expense Statement Worksheet

Here's a handy guide for figuring your expected income and expenses for one month. For a nifty note sheet, photocopy this page before you begin. Then, when you're finished, total up the cost to give yourself a head start on the "Projected Operating Budget" in Chapter 6 on page 65.

Income	
Machine sales	
Other income	
Total Monthly Income	
Expenses	
Advertising/marketing	
Bank service charges	
Commissions	
CPA/accounting	
Depreciation	
Office equipment/furnishings	
Vehicles	
Vending machines	
Insurance	
Licenses and fees	
Office expenses	
Equipment/furnishings	
Office supplies	
Rent	
Repairs/maintenance	
Telephone	
Utilities	
Payroll	
Salaries/wages	
Benefits	
Payroll taxes	
Workers' compensation	

Income and Expense Statement Worksheet, continued

Product expenses	
Cost of goods sold	
Product loss	
Professional services (including contract)	
Sales/use taxes	
Subscriptions/dues	
Travel, meals, entertainment	
Vehicle expenses	
Vehicle purchases	
Lease payments	
Loan payments—principal	
Loan payments—interest	
Maintenance and repair	
Vending Equipment Expenses	
Machine purchases	
Lease payments	
Loan payments—principal	
Loan payments—interest	
Parts and repairs	
Storage	
Delivery/moving/freight	
Other Miscellaneous Expenses	
Total monthly expenses	
Net monthly profit (loss) before taxes	
Income tax (estimated)	
Net monthly profit (loss) after taxes	

Words of
Wisdom

Although it has its idiosyncrasies, vending is really no different from any other business. To be successful in the field, it takes solid business management, old-fashioned elbow grease, plenty of persistence, and an ample dose of optimism.

Photo© Automatic Products International Ltd.

In addition to this tried-and-true wisdom, we asked the operators and experts interviewed for this book what the most important factors are for success in vending. Not surprisingly, their answers were very candid.

From a Position of Strength

When asked to name the most important factor for success, the first response from everyone who contributed to this work was, "Know what you're getting into from a hands-on perspective."

Northridge, California, full-line operator Becky P. explained the concept most eloquently. "Nobody—*nobody*—should try to go into this business without working one full year as a route person for a reputable operator. Lots of people go in, buy a business opportunity, get two weeks' training, and fall flat on their faces. The best way to get your education is by working in the trenches for a year and keeping your eyes and ears open. After three months, you may say to yourself, Am I out of my mind? Then you can give your two weeks' notice and leave. But if you've got $50,000, $100,000, or $150,000 of your life savings invested, it's not so easy to say, Boy, did I make a mistake."

Across the country from Becky's Southern California operation, veteran start-up watcher Vince Gumma of Chicago-based equipment distributor American Vending Sales, agrees. "The most successful are those who have worked for a vending operator and decide to go out on their own. They can see what's really involved in running a company."

There Is Another Way

If, for whatever reason, you decide getting a job with a vending company just isn't for you, another industry veteran offers an alternative. "Before you get into the business, come [ride along with our delivery drivers] and see what it's like," invites product distributor John Ochi of Five Star Distributors in Vernon Hills, Illinois. "We'll show you the dredges of our stops and the best. Also, with the approval of one of our operators [outside your competition area], we'll take you out and show you what it's like day to day. If you don't [get firsthand experience], you're going to be an island unto yourself. You're going to make a lot of mistakes, and it's less likely that you'll succeed."

But why would an established operator let a potential operator peer into the inner workings of his business? "Because," says Ochi, "it doesn't do anyone in this industry any good when people fail."

Give Yourself a Break

No matter how much hands-on learning you do before you paint your business name on a shingle, you're going to make mistakes. Thus, the next most important factor to your success is learning from your mistakes and moving on—and the sooner the better.

"One of the things I find is true with most businesses is they tend to get with something and stay with it," notes Burnsville, Minnesota's Wayne D., who worked his way up from a dozen snack and cigarette machines to becoming a full-line operator ready to hand over the reins to his son. "Be willing to be flexible and make the changes. Deep-six the things you make some mistakes on.

"If you make a mistake, you make a mistake," he continues. "Be willing to admit to the mistake. Otherwise, you can save pennies on one side and lose dollars on the other side. And that's a pitfall for most small businesses."

Fun Fact

Vending is historically a male-dominated industry, but Northridge, California, full-line operator Becky P. attributes her success to having a woman's touch. "Men don't look at food the way women look at food," she says. "I can't have people coming up to my food [machines] without it looking like they're coming to my house for lunch."

Be Reasonable

Equally vital to learning from your mistakes is using common sense. This is especially true in all matters related to financing and growth.

For example, as Hendersonville, Tennessee, full-line operator B.J. S. put it so succinctly in Chapter 6, borrowing money at 10 percent to purchase new vendors when the industry's ROI (return on investment) is 3 or 4 percent means you'll never have enough to pay off your debt.

Merchandise, Merchandise, Merchandise

The earlier you learn merchandising skills, the better, say our interviewees. "The object is to put a couple more of a good seller in a machine so [you] don't need to go back to this one machine every day just to fill a single column," says product broker Jim Patterson of Patterson Co. Inc. in Kenilworth, Illinois. "It's better to go back every three or four days and fill multiple machines."

"Managing that has a great deal to do with one's success," Patterson continues. "There's a fine balance between servicing too often and not servicing often enough. There's a cost to both." In the case of the former, it's wasted time, and in the latter, it's lost sales opportunities.

Be a Joiner

While many start-ups only look at the cost of dues when considering membership in an industry organization, successful ones look at the benefits.

> ### Smart Tip
> **Tip...**
>
> If you decide vending is not for you, consider retaining a professional who specializes in brokering business sales and acquisitions. Like a real estate agent, a broker will take a cut of the sales price, but in the final analysis, you're likely to gain more than you'll lose. To find a reputable broker, call the industry organization dedicated to your product specialty.

"It's absolutely important if you're starting out," assures B.J. S., who had no plans to go into vending until his father-in-law, who owned a vending business, suddenly decided to retire. "You find out what's going on in your industry and how your industry can help you." In B.J.'s case, this included learning about a tax break that cut his sales taxes from eight and a half to one and a half percent.

"Some people say, 'I don't want to socialize with my competition,' " continues the full-line Tennessee operator. "I say, the only way to know your competition is to meet them."

In addition to serving as an invaluable resource, membership in industry organizations can be a sales tool. "I can point to the

International Telecard Association (ITA) and say, 'This card issuer is a mover and shaker in ITA, and here's the ad that says so,'" says Preston, Washington, telecard operator Pat W. "I show them I'm carrying a product [made by a company] that has the professionalism to belong to the association that's on the side of the law."

Calling It Quits

At some point during your first year, assess your happiness with owning a business. Are you operating successfully? Is your quality of life fulfilling? Or is it time to try something new?

Whether or not you're profitable, the long-term success of your business rests on your happiness. Because it's a lot of work and a lot of responsibility, you might discover that you'd be happier working for someone else. Remember that everything you've learned will make you an attractive candidate. And if you'd like to stay in vending, there's plenty of industry precedent for being bought out by someone who'll pay you a handsome salary to manage a component of their organization.

Should you decide to get out, industry magazine *Automatic Merchandiser* offers some savvy advice for selling your business. First, you're not just selling vending machines. You're selling locations as well as the information you've collected about past and current locations. You may have even worked out some unique systems for servicing locations and maintaining good customer relations. All of this, and more, is valuable to a new owner.

But before you go shopping for a buyer, acquaint yourself with nondisclosure and noncompete agreements. Otherwise, during the course of selling your business, you may lose accounts to a competitor or—worse—to an unscrupulous buyer.

Determination Wins the Day

The final key ingredient for success is just plain grit. "I usually tell [new operators] that they should be prepared to put in a lot of hours and to work very hard," Gumma asserts. "It seems to be a glamorous business because of the cash [you collect from the machines], but people overlook the hard work. Vending is not something you can do five days a week from nine to five. I know successful operators who haven't had a vacation in 15 years; they may have five employees, but the owner just can't get away."

Five Star Distributors' Ochi concurs. "The typical successful vending operator is someone who's really willing to roll up their sleeves," he emphasizes. "It's a labor-intensive business. You have to lug machines up [flights] of stairs, you have to fill them anytime of day or night, and you have to burn the candle at both ends. You don't have to have technical or management skills; you can learn them. But it's a service industry—you have to do whatever it takes to satisfy the client."

▲

To this Baltimore pantyhose vending pioneer Janice M. adds, "Most successful businesspeople aren't that way because they had a lot of money [to start out with], but because they kept at it and finished what they started. You have to decide whether you want a new pair of shoes or to be successful. You can't take that money and use it to live off of. You have to use it for your business," she says. "You have to commit to finishing the project."

This winning attitude seems especially key. If you go into business with the right stuff—a willingness to learn what vending is really about, to work hard, to merchandise effectively, to satisfy your customer—and the drive to get it done, chances are you will succeed.

Appendix
Vending Business Resources

As we have repeatedly admonished, becoming a successful vending entrepreneur requires doing your homework. To help you start sleuthing, we've compiled the following resources for you to consult. Many of the sources listed were discussed in various chapters.

Although we've made every attempt to provide you with the most comprehensive and updated information, businesses and organizations do tend to move, evolve, expand, and fold. So if you discover a telephone number that has changed or an address that's different, make a note next to its entry in this Appendix and then follow the new lead. Not only will perseverance net you the knowledge you seek, but it'll mirror what you'll be doing daily as a business owner: problem-solving.

In addition to what's here, we urge you to contact the appropriate association for your intended vending specialty. There you'll find even more literature, audiocassettes, and videotapes. And get on the Web. In cyberspace, you'll locate yet more links to data, equipment, products, and oodles of friendly advice. Don't have a computer? No problem; your public library most likely does.

Now go forth, do the research, and be a success!

Associations

American Amusement Machine Association, 450 E. Higgins Rd., #201, Elk Grove Village, IL 60007-1417, (847) 290-9088, fax: (847) 290-9121, www.coin-op.org

Amusement & Music Operators Association, 450 E. Higgins Rd., #202, Elk Grove Village, IL 60007-1417, (847) 290-5320, fax: (847) 290-0409, www.amoa.com

International Telecard Association (ITA), 904 Massachusetts Ave. NE, Washington, DC 20002, (202) 544-4448, fax: (202) 547-7417, www.telecard.org, info@telecard.org

National Automatic Merchandising Association (NAMA), 20 N. Wacker Dr., #3500, Chicago, IL 60606-3102, (312) 346-0370, fax: (312) 704-4140, www.vending.org, info@vending.org

> Eastern Office: 783 Station St., Ste. 1D, Herndon, VA 20170-4607, (703) 435-1210, fax: (703) 435-6389

> Southern Office: 1640 Powers Ferry Rd. SE, Marietta, GA 30067, (770) 988-0048, fax: (770) 988-0404

> Western Office: 16030 Ventura Blvd., Encino, CA 91436-2745, (818) 783-8363, fax: (818) 783-0232

National Bulk Vendors Association, 200 N. La Salle St., #2100 Chicago, IL 60601, (312) 621-1400, fax: (312) 621-1750, www.nbva.org

National Coffee Service Association, 4000 Williamsburg Sq., Fairfax, VA 22032, (703) 273-9008, fax: (703) 273-9011

Books

A Concise History of Vending in the United States, G. Richard Schreiber, Sunrise Books, available from NAMA

Entrepreneur's business start-up guide No. 1811, *Starting Your Own Business*

Entrepreneur's business start-up guide No. 1812, *Managing Your Small Business*

Entrepreneur's business start-up guide No. 1815, *Starting & Running Your Homebased BusinessThe Ultimate Small Business Advisor*, Andi Axman, Entrepreneur Press

Vending for Investors, G. Richard Schreiber, Sunrise Books, available from American Vending Sales Inc.

The Vending Start-Up Kit, The Vending Connection, 4303 Blue Ridge Blvd., #543, Kansas City, MO 64122, (800) 956-8363, (816) 554-1534, fax: (816) 554-1016, www.vendingconnection.com

Business Opportunities

See *Entrepreneur's Annual Business Opportunity 500*

Buyer's Guides

Bluebook, Automatic Merchandiser, 1233 Janesville Ave., P.O. Box 803, Ft. Atkinson, WI 53538-0803, (920) 563-6388, fax: (920) 563-1702, www.amonline.com

International Buyers Guide, Vending Times, 1375 Broadway, 6th Fl., New York, NY 10018, (212) 302-4700, fax: (212) 221-3311

Industry Experts

Donald C. Blotner, DCB Consulting, 895 Sunwood Ct., Eagan, MN 55123-2293, (651) 452-3354, fax: (651) 452-7978, www.blumontheweb.com/dcb/index.html, blotn 001 @minter.net

Vince Gumma, American Vending Sales Inc., 750 Morse Ave., Elk Grove Village, IL 60007-5104, (847) 439-9400, fax: (847) 439-9405, TDD: (847) 439-9402, www.american vending.com, avs@americanvending.com

Jim Patterson, Patterson Co. Inc., 414 Green Bay Rd., Kenilworth, IL 60043-1097, (847) 251-2525, fax: (847) 251-3083

John Ochi, Five Star Distributors Inc., 220 Fairway Dr., Vernon Hills, IL 60061, (847) 680-9900, fax: (847) 680-9910

Pamphlets

Business Opportunities: Avoiding Vending Machine and Display Rack Scams, Federal Trade Commission, Bureau of Consumer Protection Office of Consumers & Business Education, Washington, DC, November 1996, (877) 382-4357, (202) 326-3650, www.ftc.gov

The Future of the Vending and Foodservice Industry 1998-2013, National Automatic Merchandising Association, 1998

Key Indicators to Success: Operating Ratio Report, National Automatic Merchandising Association

Tips on Automatic Vending Machines, Council of Better Business Bureaus, Arlington, VA, 1993

Publications

Automatic Merchandiser, 1233 Janesville Ave., P.O. Box 803, Ft. Atkinson, WI 53538-0803, (920) 563-6388, fax: (920) 563-1702, www.amonline.com

Canadian Vending, 222 Argyle Ave., Delhi, ON N4B 2Y2, Canada, (519) 582-2513, fax: (519) 582-4040

Intele-Card News, 10200 Grogan's Mill Rd., #150, The Woodlands, TX 77380, (281) 298-1431, fax: (281) 362-1771, www.intelecard.com, info@intelecard.com

Play Meter, 6600 Fleur De Lis, New Orleans, LA 70124, (504) 488-7003, fax: (504) 488- 7083, www.playmeter.com

Replay, 22157 Claredon St., Woodland Hills, CA 91365, (818) 347-3820, fax: (818) 347-2112

St. Beat, 85 N. Third St., #6E, Brooklyn, NY 11211, (718) 388-4370, fax: (718) 388-5859, SbeatMail@aol.com

Telecard World, P.O. Box 42190, Houston, TX 77242, (713) 974-5252, fax: (713) 974-5459

Vending & OCS, 4016 Flower Rd., #440A, Atlanta, GA 30360, (770) 451-2345 fax: (770) 457-0748

Vending Times, 1375 Broadway, 6th Fl., New York, NY 10018, (212) 302-4700, fax: (212) 221-3311

Research Firms

Hudson Analytics Inc., 5395 Emerson Way, Indianapolis, IN 46226, (317) 549-4132

Technomic Inc., 300 S. Riverside Plaza, Chicago, IL 60606, (312) 876-0004

Successful Vending Business Operators

A Matter of Taste, Rebecca Palazzola, 19145 Parthenia St., Ste. K, Northridge, CA 91324, (818) 993-7140

EasyCall Inc., Patricia M. Williams, P.O. Box 535, Preston, WA 98050, (425) 222-7576

McLean Machines & Co. Inc., Janice L. McLean, P.O. Box 29147, Baltimore, MD 21205, (888) 515-0366

Midwest Vending Inc., Wayne Doyle, 11750 Millpond Ave., Burnsville, MN 55337, (612) 707-1990

Van Vending Service Inc., Bjorn "B.J." R. Svedin, One Candy Ln., P.O. Box 586, Hendersonville, TN 37077, (615) 824-2000, www.vanvend.com

Suppliers—Consumables

Five Star Distributors Inc. (consumables distributor), 220 Fairway Dr., Vernon Hills, IL 60061, (847) 680-9900, fax: (847) 680-9910

Nabisco Inc. (food products manufacturer), 7 Campus Dr., P.O. Box 3111, Parsippany, NJ 07054-0311, (800) 852-9393, (973) 682-6880, fax: (973) 682-7476, www.nabisco.com

Patterson Co. Inc. (product broker), 414 Green Bay Rd., Kenilworth, IL 60043-1097, (847) 251-2525, fax: (847) 251-3083

Vendors Purchasing Council (purchasing cooperative), 204 Laird St., Ste. A, Greensburg, PA 15601, (724) 838-8977, www.vpcoop.com

Suppliers—Equipment

American Vending Sales Inc. (vending machine distributor), 750 Morse Ave., Elk Grove Village, IL 60007-5104, (847) 439-9400, fax: (847) 439-9405, TDD: (847) 439-9402, www.americanvending.com, avs@americanvending.com

Automatic Products International, Ltd. (food vending machine manufacturer), 75 W. Plato Blvd., St. Paul, MN 55107-2095, (800) 523-8363, (651) 224-4391, fax: (651) 224-3609, www.automaticproducts.com

Technik Manufacturing Inc. (telecard vending machine manufacturer), 1005 17th St., Columbus, NE 68601, (888) 832-4645, (402) 564-3191, fax: (402) 564-0406, www.technikmfg.com, technik@megavision.com

Glossary

Bank: two or more vending machines in a row; also refers to a route person's change fund.

Belt: the part of a vending machine that carries the product on a circular, revolving belt to the point of delivery.

Bill changer: see *changer*.

Bin: the individual dispensing space allotted for a product in a food vendor, most commonly used by the telecard industry to describe the place where telecards are stacked up to await dispensing; see also synonymous terms *column* and *spiral*.

Broker: another term for independent sales representative. Brokers represent manufacturers that are too small to—or choose not to—maintain their own internal sales force. Although they don't actually sell you products, they're an important source of information and leads for purchasing products at competitive prices.

Bulk operator: specializes in vending machines offering gum balls, trinkets, and charms, usually at one cent or five cents with larger offerings at $.10 and $.25.

Cash & carry: refers to a purchasing system that is between wholesale and retail. At wholesale, the quantity minimum is generally a

▲

case (box) of a given product at a significant discount from retail. Item selection is done from a catalog, and purchases are delivered by the wholesaler to the buyer. At a cash & carry, the minimum quantity is a single unit, but merchandise is sold in a no-frills manner out of cut-open cases; items are priced below retail. Generally, cash & carries offer a further discount if a case quantity is purchased. The term cash & carry describes the wholesale/retail hybrid system where customers (most often businesses) must pay cash or cash-equivalent, such as credit card (rather than being invoiced later), and carry purchases out themselves (rather than have them delivered).

Category management: an objective system of merchandising products to maximize sales.

Catering truck: a truck designed to dispense hot and cold food and beverages as well as sundry items; generally services installations not large enough to support a vending or manual food-service operation; can provide an additional service for a large plant. Food and beverages are prepared in a central commissary. Sales are handled by the driver.

Changer: a machine that makes change for coins or bills without a vend of merchandise (also called a bill changer).

Client: the person or company who contracts with you to place vendors at their location. A client can also be a customer, but only when he or she is making a purchase from your machine.

Coin mechanism: the mechanism within a vending machine that dispenses change or counts coins deposited.

Cold call: a sales technique that involves telephoning or personally visiting a prospect who has no prior knowledge of you or your business.

Column: the individual dispensing space allotted for a product in a food vendor; most commonly used when referring to a canned beverage machine where cans are stacked in individual columns to await dispensing; see also synonymous terms *bin* and *spiral*.

Commissary: specialized food production facility from which the operator serves multiple locations; used primarily for vended food installations, mobile catering trucks, and social catering. Facilities may range from small family-run operations to modern plants that include bakeries and mass production equipment.

Commissions: payment of a percentage of vending sales by the vending machine service company to the client organization for the privilege of operating on its premises. Payments are usually made monthly. Rates differ according to size of location, types of products vended, and competitive factors.

Contract vending: the installation and operation of vending machines by a private contractor who retains title to his vending equipment while performing his services.

Cooperative (purchasing): an association of operators, usually small businesses, who join together for purchasing purposes. By soliciting distributors as a group, cooperatives assure a certain annual volume and therefore command a lower price.

Cup mechanism: a device that feeds cups in a drink vending machine.

Customer: a person who makes purchases from a vending machine. Often, a customer is an employee at your client's business.

Cycle: the length of time a machine takes to vend one unit.

Cycle menu: a food menu that repeats itself after a certain interval of time. Most common cycles are two-week, four-week, 20-day, and six-week menus.

Décor: the nonfunctional trim and decorative work installed around vending machines.

Delivery receipt: see *route card*.

Distributor: companies that sell equipment and consumables directly to operators. Distributors carry the products of a wide variety of manufacturers.

Drum: horizontal rotating shelves in a machine.

Employee feeding: see *in-plant feeding*.

Fixed level: see *par*.

Food-service contract: a contract awarded on the basis of the specifications for proposals and the submitted proposal.

Free-standing machine: a single machine installation, distinguished from a bank.

Free-vend: a machine purposely adjusted to vend product at no charge.

Full-line: complete food and refreshment service through vending machines.

HMR (home meal replacement): meals, or meal components, that are prepared by a business for in-home consumption. The HMR market is characterized as consumers interested in the taste and ambiance of home dining without spending the time or effort on food preparation and cleanup.

Income statement (or income and expense statement): a report of all collections and disbursements for a business during a specific period, often monthly, used to determine net profit/loss.

In-plant feeding: any type of food service performed in an industrial or institutional setting; a general term that makes no distinction between independent contractors and company operated facilities.

▲

International Telecard Association: see *ITA.*

ITA: International Telecard Association; the umbrella association for the pre-paid telecard industry, which includes vended, over-the-counter, and all other sales types in the telecard industry.

Jackpot: a malfunction within a coin/ bill changer or vending machine whereby part or all of the change and/or product in the machine is incorrectly dispensed.

Joint replenishment: the ability to buy two or more items from the same supplier on a single purchase order.

Legs: a leveling device on the bottom of a vending machine.

Location manager: a representative of the vending company who is permanently assigned to one particular account.

Location-owned operations: services similar to the contractor's but owned and operated by a college or factory on its own premises by its own staff; includes location-owned cafeteria, dining, and vending operations.

Machine settlement: see *par out.*

Manual food service: conventional cafeteria, short-order, or table service where the customer is served by manual delivery rather than by vending machines.

Manufacturer: a company that produces vending equipment or consumables. Some manufacturers sell to operators directly, but most sell through distributors.

Marginal: applied to vending machine locations where traffic of potential customers is so small as to make vending machine placement feasible only if equipment is fully depreciated, or the placement fills a gap in route scheduling or is subsidized by the location so that operating costs are reduced to the point where the operator can make a profit.

Merchandising: the process of determining the exact brand, color, flavor, size, type, quantity, and placement of products consumers want to buy and then presenting the products to them in a manner that encourages them to do so. This can be accomplished anecdotally, by passively observing which products are being purchased, or systematically, by actively employing a measurable system often referred to as category management.

Meter: a machine-attached device that records the number of vending cycles.

Mixed route (or full-line route): a route that handles several types of products.

NAMA: National Automatic Merchandising Association; the umbrella trade association of the vending and contract food industry.

National Automatic Merchandising Association: see *NAMA*.

Net worth: a person or business's assets minus liabilities. Assets are generally tangible property such as buildings, vehicles, equipment, furniture, machinery, etc. Liabilities are generally intangible, such as loans, leases, or credit card debt.

Operating statement (or operating budget): an annual version of an income and expense statement used to determine actual net profit/loss or projected financial receipts and disbursements.

Operator: someone who owns a vending machine business. If you're reading this book, you're interested in becoming an operator. In the industry, the term vendor is also used to mean operator, but generally, vendor is the term for a vending machine. In this work, operator is always used to refer to the owner of a vending business, and vendor is always used to refer to a vending machine.

Par (or fixed level): the fixed inventory established for an individual machine.

Par out (or machine settlement): 1. a term being replaced by servicing, or the process of collecting sales proceeds (coin/ currency), and maintaining and filling a machine; 2. the process by which the merchandise and sales in a vending machine at any point in time are reconciled to the par, or fixed level, of the machine to determine if any overage or shortage exists. Sales plus the retail value of merchandise remaining in the machine should equal exactly the retail value of the par or fixed level.

Planogram: a simple diagram of an individual vendor with a specific product assigned to each spiral. Historically, as vendor capacity grew (most machines now include 40 or more spirals), more sophisticated selection and placement of products (aka merchandising) became necessary for profitability, and planogramming was born.

Pro forma income: an anticipated operating statement of potential activity in a food-service location.

Proposal: a complete description of the type of food service to be provided.

Rehab (or renovate): to rebuild a changer or vending machine; also refers to the rebuilt machine.

Request for proposal: see *RFP*.

Resident vend: a vending operation at a client location that has one or more resident route persons or hostesses. It is thus distinguished from a location on a route, which is serviced by traveling route personnel.

Return on investment: see *ROI*.

Return on sales: the amount of money earned after taxes by a company at a particular location in relation to the sales of that location; usually expressed in a percentage form.

▲

RFP: request for proposal; a request to various companies to submit proposals to provide food and vending services.

ROI: return on investment; the amount of money earned after taxes by a company at a particular location in relation to the total dollar investment required to operate in that location; usually expressed in a percentage form.

Route: a sequence of locations serviced by a traveling route person. The number of locations in a route is completely specific to each vending business. For example, you'd have two routes if you have 15 machines, which you serviced each week, going to seven one day and eight another. However, you'd also have two routes if you had 70 machines, of which you serviced 50 machines each week (ten each day) and your employee services 20 (four each day).

Route card: a card on which a route person keeps all manner of data about each vending machine he or she services (what sold, how much sold, what products were put into the machine, how much money was collected, etc.).

Route accountability: a bookkeeping system whereby the retail value of merchandise issuances to a route person is equated to cash sales turned in by that route person to determine if overages or shortages exist on his route.

Route person: the individual who services one or more vending locations.

Route structure: the sequence in which a group of vending accounts is serviced by a route person.

Route vend: a group of individual vending locations serviced by a route person; today, the more commonly used term is route or route structure.

Satellite: a site removed from the main location but serviced by the same resident vend.

Servicing (or servicing a machine): the process of collecting coins/currency, cleaning, maintaining, repairing, and, most importantly, filling a vendor; in other words, servicing machines is what you do every day on a route.

Shelf life: the length of time a product will keep without deterioration that makes it unsaleable.

SKU: stock-keeping unit; a number assigned to a product by a manufacturer and used to identify that product; virtually every retail product in the United States has a SKU.

Specifications for proposals: a uniform set of specifications to ensure a reasonable basis of comparison for various proposals.

Spiral: the individual dispensing space allotted for a product in a food vendor; because today's snack machines move products forward via a mechanism shaped like a spiral, the term has been adopted to mean any individual offering, snack, sandwich, soda, etc.; see also synonymous terms *bin* and *column*.

Standard menu: a menu that includes a certain entree served with certain appetizers, vegetables, desserts, etc.

Stock-keeping unit: see *SKU.*

Subsidy contract: a contract that guarantees the operator a specific level of profit, normally a fixed fee or a percentage of sales. When the operation doesn't generate the guaranteed revenue, the operator bills the client for the balance. If the profit generated is greater than the contractual amount, the excess is generally returned to the client.

Supplementary vending: small banks or individual pieces of vending machines scattered throughout a location to provide back-up service for a more complete centralized manual or automatic food-service operation.

Telecards: the industry term for pre-paid phone cards. Pre-paid phone cards come in set dollar denominations, often $5, $10, and $20. The amount of minutes on a card varies depending on the card issuer and location called. Generally, any card can be used to call anywhere in the world. However, cards are specialized and usually offer inexpensive rates to a particular country.

Throw: the amount of product, usually liquid, dispensed per vending cycle.

Vend: the delivery of a single unit of merchandise.

Vending (automatic vending): retail selling of merchandise and services by means of coin-operated dispensers.

Vending cafeteria: a location where all food and beverages are dispensed through vending machines.

Vendor: the abbreviated term for vending machine. In the industry, vendor also sometimes means operator, but in this book we keep the two terms strictly separate.

Index

▲